$\mathscr{P}$ROFILES IN WORLD HISTORY

Significant Events and the People Who Shaped Them

Volume 3: *The Crusades to Building Empires in the Americas, 1095-1500*

Crusades and Mongol Expansion
Saladin, Genghis Khan, Innocent III, Alexius V

Religion and Reason in the Middle Ages
Averroës, Maimonides, Thomas Aquinas

Beginning of Constitutional Government in England
Thomas Becket, King John

Muslim Influences on Empires in West Africa
Al-Bakri, Sundiata, Mansa Musa

Exploring the East
Marco Polo, William of Rubrouck, Ibn Battutah

Building Empires in Europe and Asia
Timur Lenk, Mehmed II, Ivan the Great, Babur

Building Empires in the Americas
Topa Inca Yupanqui, Moctezuma I

Volume 4: *The Age of Discovery to Industrial Revolution, 1400-1830*

Beginnings of the Age of Discovery
Cheng Ho, Vasco da Gama, Jacques Cartier

Religious Reform
Desiderius Erasmus, Guru Nanak, Ignatius of Loyola, Martin Luther

Revival of Science
Leonardo da Vinci, Tycho Brahe, Johannes Kepler

Revival of Literature
Francis Bacon, Miguel de Cervantes, William Shakespeare

Rise of Nationalism
Suleiman the Magnificent, Hideyoshi Toyotomi,   therine the Great

Enlightenment
John Locke, Voltaire, Jean-Jacques Rousseau

Industrial Revolution
Charles Townshend, Richard Arkwright, James

ti.   n inside back cover)

PROFILES IN
WORLD HISTORY

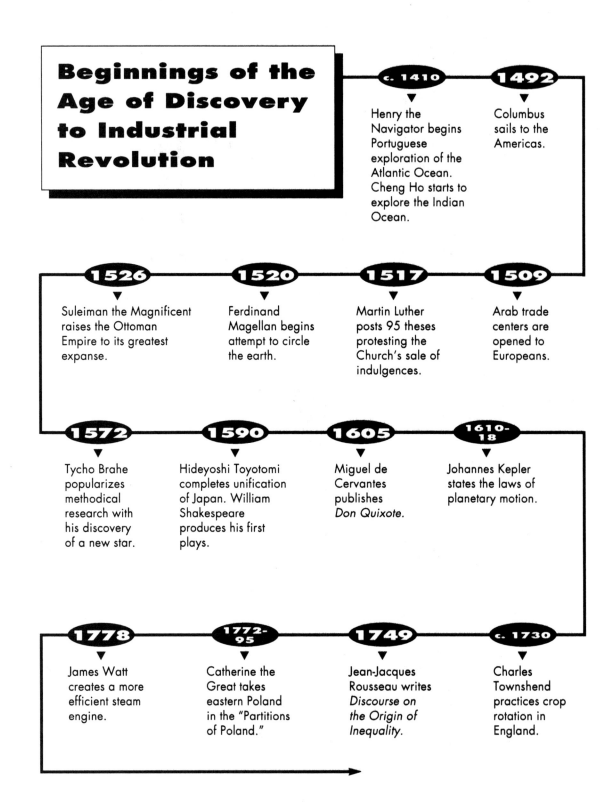

Beginnings of the Age of Discovery to Industrial Revolution

c. 1410
Henry the Navigator begins Portuguese exploration of the Atlantic Ocean. Cheng Ho starts to explore the Indian Ocean.

1492
Columbus sails to the Americas.

1526
Suleiman the Magnificent raises the Ottoman Empire to its greatest expanse.

1520
Ferdinand Magellan begins attempt to circle the earth.

1517
Martin Luther posts 95 theses protesting the Church's sale of indulgences.

1509
Arab trade centers are opened to Europeans.

1572
Tycho Brahe popularizes methodical research with his discovery of a new star.

1590
Hideyoshi Toyotomi completes unification of Japan. William Shakespeare produces his first plays.

1605
Miguel de Cervantes publishes *Don Quixote.*

1610-18
Johannes Kepler states the laws of planetary motion.

1778
James Watt creates a more efficient steam engine.

1772-95
Catherine the Great takes eastern Poland in the "Partitions of Poland."

1749
Jean-Jacques Rousseau writes *Discourse on the Origin of Inequality.*

c. 1730
Charles Townshend practices crop rotation in England.

PROFILES IN WORLD HISTORY

Significant Events and the People
Who Shaped Them

4

Beginnings of the Age of Discovery to Industrial Revolution

JOYCE MOSS
and
GEORGE WILSON

AN IMPRINT OF GALE RESEARCH
AN INTERNATIONAL THOMSON PUBLISHING COMPANY

℘ROFILES IN WORLD HISTORY

Significant Events and the People Who Shaped Them

Volume 4: Beginnings of the Age of Discovery to Industrial Revolution

Joyce Moss and George Wilson

Staff

Carol DeKane Nagel, *U•X•L Developmental Editor*
Julie L. Carnagie, *U•X•L Assistant Editor*
Thomas L. Romig, *U•X•L Publisher*

Shanna P. Heilveil, *Production Assistant*
Evi Seoud, *Assistant Production Manager*
Mary Beth Trimper, *Production Director*

Barbara A. Wallace, *Permissions Associate (Pictures)*

Mary Krzewinski, *Cover and Page Designer*
Cynthia Baldwin, *Art Director*

The Graphix Group, *Typesetting*

∞™ This book is printed on acid-free paper that meets the minimum requirements of American National Standard for Information Sciences—Permanence Paper for Printed Library Materials, ANSI Z39.48-1984.

ISBN 0-7876-0464-X (Set)
ISBN 0-7876-0465-8 (v. 1)   ISBN 0-7876-0469-0 (v. 5)
ISBN 0-7876-0466-6 (v. 2)   ISBN 0-7876-0470-4 (v. 6)
ISBN 0-7876-0467-4 (v. 3)   ISBN 0-7876-0471-2 (v. 7)
ISBN 0-7876-0468-2 (v. 4)   ISBN 0-7876-0472-0 (v. 8)

Printed in the United States of America

I(T)P™ U·X·L is an imprint of Gale Research,
an International Thomson Publishing Company.
ITP logo is a trademark under license.

Contents

v

Reader's Guide

Profiles in World History: Significant Events and the People Who Shaped Them presents the life stories of more than 175 individuals who have played key roles in world history. The biographies are clustered around 50 broad events, ranging from the Rise of Eastern Religions and Philosophies to the Expansion of World Powers, from Industrial Revolution to Winning African Independence. Each biography—complete in itself—contributes a singular outlook regarding an event; when taken as cluster, the biographies provide a variety of views and experiences, thereby offering a broad perspective on events that shaped the world.

Those whose stories are told in *Profiles in World History* meet one or more of the following criteria. The individuals:

- Represent viewpoints or groups involved in a major world event
- Directly affected the outcome of the event
- Exemplify a role played by common citizens in that event

Format

Profiles in World History volumes are arranged by chapter. Each chapter focuses on one particular event and opens with an overview and detailed time line of the event that places it in historical context. Following are biographical profiles of two to five diverse individuals who played active roles in the event.

Each biographical profile is divided into four sections:

- **Personal Background** provides details that predate and anticipate the individual's involvement in the event

• **Participation** describes the role played by the individual in the event and its impact on his or her life

• **Aftermath** discusses effects of the individual's actions and subsequent relevant events in the person's life

• **For More Information** provides sources for further reading on the individual

Additionally, sidebars containing interesting details about the events and individuals profiled are interspersed throughout the text.

Additional Features

Portraits, illustrations, and maps as well as excerpts from primary source materials are included in *Profiles in World History* to help bring history to life. Sources of all quoted material are cited parenthetically within the text, and complete bibliographic information is listed at the end of each biography. A full bibliography of scholarly sources consulted in preparing each volume appears in each book's back matter.

Cross references are made in the entries, directing readers to other entries within the volume that are connected in some way to the person under scrutiny. Additionally, each volume ends with a subject index, while Volume 8 concludes with a cumulative subject index, providing easy access to the people and events mentioned throughout *Profiles in World History.*

Comments and Suggestions

We welcome your comments on this work as well as your suggestions for individuals to be featured in future editions of *Profiles in World History.* Please write: Editors, *Profiles in World History,* U·X·L, 835 Penobscot Bldg., Detroit, Michigan 48226-4094; fax to 313-961-6348; or call toll-free: 1-800-877-4253.

Acknowledgments

The editors would like to thank the many people involved in the preparation of *Profiles in World History*.

For guidance in the choice of events and personalities, we are grateful to Ross Dunn, Professor of History at the University of California at San Diego, and David Smith, Professor of History at California Polytechnic University at Pomona. We're thankful to Professor Smith for his careful review of the entire series and his guidance toward key sources of information about personalities and events.

We deeply appreciate the writers who compiled data and contributed to the biographies: Diane Ahrens, Bill Boll, Quesiyah Ali Chavez, Charity-Jean Conklin, Mario Cutajar, Craig Hinkel, Hillary Manning, Lawrence Orr, Phillip T. Slattery, Colin Wells, and Susan Yun. We'd especially like to thank Jamie Mohn and Cheryl Steets for their careful attention to the manuscript.

Thanks also to the copy editors and proofreaders, Sonia Benson, Barbara C. Bigelow, Betz Des Chenes, Robert Griffin, Rob Nagel, and Paulette Petrimoulx, for their careful attention to style and detail. Special thanks to Margaret M. Johnson, Judith Kass, and John F. Petruccione for researching the illustrations and maps.

And, finally, thanks to Carol Nagel of U·X·L for overseeing the production of the series.

Picture Credits

The photographs and illustrations appearing in *Profiles in World History: Significant Events and the People Who Shaped Them,* Volume 4: *Beginnings of the Age of Discovery to Industrial Revolution* were received from the following sources:

On the cover: Leonardo da Vinci; **The Bettmann Archive:** Jacques Cartier; Catherine the Great.

Archive Photos: pp. 119, 152; **The Bettmann Archive:** pp. 10, 23, 28, 41, 43, 107, 163, 187, 192; **The Granger Collection:** pp. 2, 15, 20, 26, 37, 56, 64, 70, 113, 115, 117, 127, 130, 135, 145, 164, 172, 194; **Popperfoto:** p. 5.

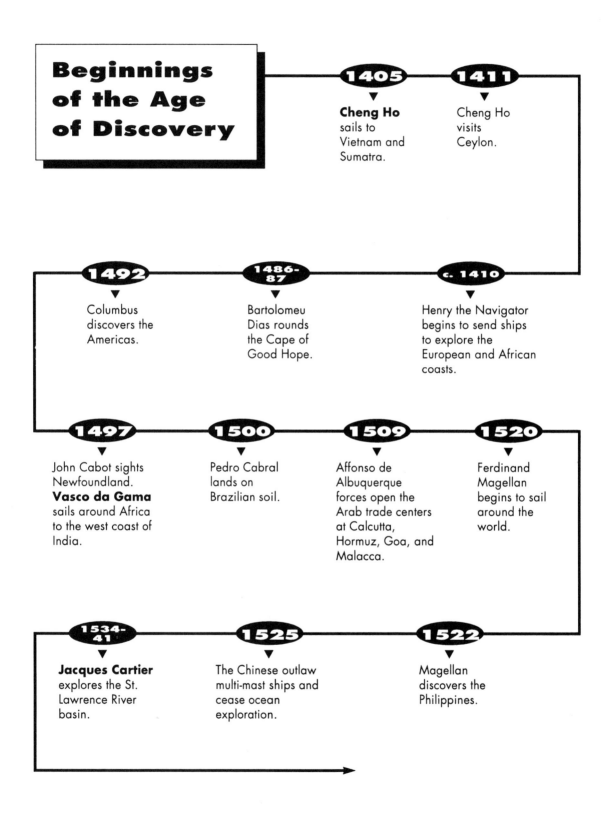

Beginnings of the Age of Discovery

1405
▼
Cheng Ho sails to Vietnam and Sumatra.

1411
▼
Cheng Ho visits Ceylon.

1492
▼
Columbus discovers the Americas.

1486-87
▼
Bartolomeu Dias rounds the Cape of Good Hope.

c. 1410
▼
Henry the Navigator begins to send ships to explore the European and African coasts.

1497
▼
John Cabot sights Newfoundland. **Vasco da Gama** sails around Africa to the west coast of India.

1500
▼
Pedro Cabral lands on Brazilian soil.

1509
▼
Affonso de Albuquerque forces open the Arab trade centers at Calcutta, Hormuz, Goa, and Malacca.

1520
▼
Ferdinand Magellan begins to sail around the world.

1534-41
▼
Jacques Cartier explores the St. Lawrence River basin.

1525
▼
The Chinese outlaw multi-mast ships and cease ocean exploration.

1522
▼
Magellan discovers the Philippines.

BEGINNINGS
OF THE AGE
OF DISCOVERY

By the beginning of the fifteenth century, the riches of the East were well known. Muslim and European traders had established trade relations with China and much of Africa. Three main routes—all equally dangerous and difficult—connected Europe with southwestern Asia. The first spanned northward across the Middle East, by land or sea around the Black Sea, then north of the Caspian Sea; the second took traders directly across Syria, past the Black Sea and through Afghanistan; the third route followed the Nile River through Egypt, crossed the Red Sea, and then continued northeast to China.

Risks of losing life or property along these routes was great. Some kingdoms along the way demanded tolls for the use of trails that ran through their lands. Venice, controlling commerce around the Adriatic Sea, threatened people passing through their trade area with a strong navy. Bandits camped along each route, threatening to steal trade goods passing east or west.

China. The Indian Ocean was a treacherous trade route for Asian ships. Chinese trade vessels (referred to as "junks") traded all along the continent's coast and in Arab ports. The ocean was given to wild and destructive weather changes. In addition, pirates were quick to attack trade ships and steal property.

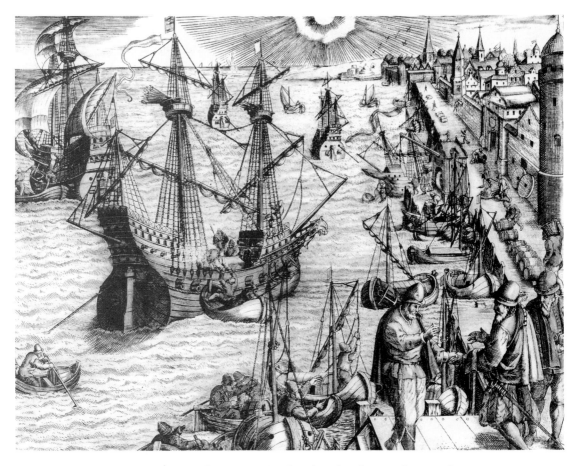

▲ A 1592 line engraving by Theodor de Bry of an exploratory voyage to the New World departing from Lisbon harbor.

Still, merchants from both the East and West were eager for the wealth that came from trade; in the early 1400s, explorers from each end began to search for safer ways to the trade centers. The emperors of China's Ming dynasty (the family that ruled from 1368 to 1644) chose faithful servants to travel the oceans in search of both trade and tribute. Chinese junks sailed from the ports near Beijing (Peking) to trade with or conquer more of the mainland and then journeyed to distant places in the Indian Ocean, including Vietnam, Harms, and the island-state of Sri Lanka.

Cheng Ho, a eunuch in the Chinese court, rose to become admiral of the emperor's private navy. In charge of multi-masted junks considered massive for the time, for more than a quarter of a century Ho sailed from port to port showing off his great might and persuading people by threat of force to trade or agree to submit to the Chinese emperor. Ho's measurements of sea routes and distances between ports around the Indian Ocean—including some as far away as Persia (present-day Iran)—helped future travelers navigate their way to the East.

European exploration. Meanwhile, a new obstacle to land travel was arising for the Europeans. The Ottoman Turks began to take charge of a large part of the Middle East, creating the potential for more problems for traders. A water route to the East was thought to exist, and European monarchs began a sea search for new paths to Asia's wealth.

After beginning exploration under the direction of Henry the Navigator (the son of a Portuguese ruler), various seamen set out from Portugal and Spain and then from England and France in search of a waterway east. They often found the unexpected. **Vasco da Gama** sailed south in his search, rounding the southern point of the African coast that Bartolomeu Dias had discovered a year earlier. He eventually reached the coast of India. A few years earlier Christopher Columbus sailed west, thinking he would find a more direct waterway to China. Instead, he reached the Dominican Republic and opened the Americas to European exploration. After these discoveries, **Jacques Cartier,** a Frenchman, explored routes farther west with no success, but during his travels he discovered Canada. Venetian pilot John Cabot sailed from England in search of a passage in the north. Each of these navigators opened new lands to be explored—and sometimes exploited—by the Europeans.

The Portuguese. In the early 1500s Portugal established a stronghold in India and sent Affonso de Albuquerque to govern its trade center there. By that time guns had been developed and tested. Albuquerque used the new weapons to bombard Calcutta, Hormuz, Gao, and Malacca, thus establishing the first major European trade network around the Indian Ocean. By 1525 the Portuguese had such a firm hold on trade in the region that the Chinese abandoned their sea explorations and even destroyed their largest ocean-going vessels. Within little more than two hundred years, nearly all the continents and major islands had been charted and mapped.

Cheng Ho

c. 1371-c. 1434

Personal Background

Early life. Cheng Ho (also spelled Zheng He) was born Ma Ho in Kunyang, in China's southern Yunnan province. His parents were Muslims of Mongol-Arab heritage. At an early age, Ho was chosen by the emperor of the Ming dynasty, or ruling family, for service in the court. Emperors in that era were considered to be "sons of heaven" and therefore entitled to the best of earthly delights, from rich foods to the most beautiful and intelligent women. Imperial harems of up to several thousand women were often kept for the pleasure of the ruler. Some men of the palace, usually eunuchs, were chosen to be protectors of these concubines; these men were castrated as young boys to ensure that they would not become sexually involved with the women.

Eunuchs frequently became personal advisers and private counselors to the emperor. Although their legal status was of the lowest class, eunuchs wielded great influence, manipulating weak rulers or adding to the powers of strong ones. Cheng Ho entered this service at the age of ten. Over the next decade, he distinguished himself in battle against the Mongols under the command of the emperor's uncle, Chu Ti.

Supply and demand. In 1402 Chu Ti overthrew his nephew and became the new Ming emperor. As was the custom, he then took a new name, Yongle (or Yung Lo). Yongle promoted Ho to the

樓舡

▲ The stern of an early Ming freighter; Cheng Ho's first duty as admiral was to oversee the building of ships for the emperor.

Event: China's exploration of Africa and the Near East.

Role: A brilliant statesman, strategist, and sailor, Cheng Ho directed seven major ocean voyages that established Chinese power and dominance in the Indian Ocean. These voyages forged cultural, political, and economic links binding three continents.

rank of grand eunuch and gave him the surname Cheng (or Zheng) in recognition of his assistance in the revolt. Three years later the emperor commissioned Cheng Ho to search for Chu Yun-Wen, the former ruler. The grand eunuch had by this time become admiral of the emperor's private navy.

Ho's voyages also served economic purposes. The breakup of the Mongol empire in Asia (1260-1368) had severed the caravan trade routes that formerly served the Chinese court. Trade was profitable, creating jobs, tariffs, and taxes; many ships sailed along the coast of China to establish trading routes by sea. In addition, the emperor was fond of exotic gifts from other countries.

Gold, Frankincense, and Myrrh

Confucianism, China's leading philosophy, considered trade to be extravagant and unnecessary—especially since the people who benefited most from it were already the wealthy class. Ho's adventures created a deep rivalry between officials, who saw trade as a moral problem, and the eunuchs, who were called on to carry out its functions.

Some historians regard Cheng Ho's missions as glorified shopping sprees, focusing on luxury items. Some of the items Cheng Ho traded suggest that this is true. Chinese materials such as gold, silver, lacquered pieces, and porcelain were traded for pearls and gemstones, fragrant woods, gum resin, art objects, incense, perfumes such as ambergris and myrrh, ivory tusks, rhinoceros horns, and tortoise shell.

In addition, there are records of gifts of exotic animals for the imperial zoo: a celestial horse (zebra), a celestial stag (oryx), a camel crane (ostrich), lions, and tigers. The giraffe was believed to be the mythical ch'i-lin; its appearance was a favorable omen, signifying the righteousness of the emperor.

Participation:
China's Exploration of Africa and the Near East

Cheng Ho's navy. Cheng Ho's first duty as admiral was to oversee the building of ships for the emperor. Chinese traders had sailed the Indian Ocean for centuries in small trade ships. Cheng Ho supervised the construction of some of the largest and strongest vessels in the region. Until the discovery of a rudderpost from one of Cheng Ho's "jewel ships" in 1962, reports of the size of Chinese craft were thought to be exaggerated. On average, they were 450 feet long and carried a crew of about seven hundred. Bamboo mat sails allowed captains to travel in most any wind; oars were used only in dead calm. Each ship was armed and armored against attack and equipped with conveniences such as four decks and cabins with key locks and closets. In addition, the

▲ **Cheng Ho was in charge of massive multi-masted junks that attracted foreign admiration and awe.**

great ships had dual pulley-drawn stone anchors; a stern post rudder; a hull divided into buoyant, watertight compartments; and as many as nine masts. China's great junks attracted foreign admiration and awe and are noted in the journals of great travelers such as Marco Polo, Ibn Battutah, and Ordoric of Pordenone.

Trade and war. Cheng Ho's ships were equipped for war and were among the largest and strongest in the world. In 1405 his great fleet sailed southward, stopping at Champa (now Vietnam) and Sumatra. The writer Ming-shih later said:

> From Champa the Chinese envoys visited one country after another. They read the imperial decree that demanded the sub-

mission of the kingdoms they visited and rewarded generously those rulers who agreed to submit. As for those who chose not to obey, force was used to assure their compliance. (Ming-shih in Li, p. 279)

Taking control. Cheng Ho shifted deftly between his duties as ambassador and admiral. In his first display of military might at Palembang in 1406, his navy defeated the pirate king Chen-Tsu-i, who had been raiding merchants in the Chinese settlement. He cleverly agreed to surrender but planned a secret second attack, thus capturing the pirate king and sending him back to the capital at Nanking for execution. Rulers of other nations were later taken prisoner and sent to the emperor to swear their allegiance to China on the threat of similar fates.

Homeward bound in 1411, Cheng Ho stopped at Ceylon (present-day Sri Lanka) to revisit local Buddhist shrines and temples. Alagonakkara, the king of the Sinhalese (Sri Lanka's primary ethnic group), invited the troops inland to his palace, demanding gifts of gold and silk. Meanwhile, Alagonakkara's troops were ordered to sink the docked ships. Cheng Ho took advantage of the army's absence and personally led two thousand soldiers in a surprise attack on the unprotected city. Ho captured the royal family and their advisers, then fought his way back to the coast to rescue his ships.

Ships of Cheng Ho and Vasco da Gama

Cheng Ho is sometimes compared with Portuguese explorer Vasco da Gama. Both were court employees chosen to become admirals of fleets exploring trade routes, but there was little similarity in their equipment.

Cheng Ho's first excursion:

- 63 ships each carrying a crew of 500 to 700
- Largest ship about 300 feet long
- Capacity of each ship between 500 and 2,500 tons

Vasco da Gama's first excursion:

- Four ships and a crew of 160
- Largest ship carried 120 tons of goods
- Capacities of other ships between 50 and 100 tons

In his battles, Ho subscribed to the Chinese idea of victory without vengeance. In contrast to the cruelty of the later conquerors, he treated prisoners with kindness and respect, returning them home after they pledged submission to Chinese rule. In this way, through war and trade, Cheng Ho expanded the area over which the Ming emperor ruled.

Trade and tribute. During his lifetime, Cheng Ho completed seven voyages that came to represent a unique period in world history. Ho felt that his adventures were guided by heaven, so he did not seek to establish patterns of slavery, commercial venture, religious conversion, or colonization. An attitude of tolerance and mutual exchange shaped China's foreign affairs at the time.

By the early part of the fifteenth century, Ho was aided in his travels by practical science. The Chinese were already far advanced in the fields of navigation and geography. Ho used navigation tools and ideas that had been developed two hundred years earlier: "The shipmaster, to ascertain his geographic position by night, looks at the stars; by day he looks at the sun; in dark weather he looks at the south-pointing needle" (Mirsky, p. 242).

Aftermath

Cheng Ho died on the last of the seven voyages at the age of sixty-three, and his body was delivered to Nanking, China, for burial.

Enduring effects. Some of Cheng Ho's navigational charts were included in *Treatment on Armament Technology* (1628); the author's note reads that the "maps record carefully and correctly the distances of the road and the various countries and I have inserted them for the information of posterity and as a memento of military achievements" (Mirsky, p. 252). Outside China, Cheng Ho was regarded as a legend; a temple in Thailand still offers sacrifices in his honor.

Isolationist ideals. Soon after Cheng Ho's last voyage, the Chinese forces that favored an agricultural economy over one of

---

Voyages of the Emperor's Navy

Admiral Cheng Ho directed great voyages for the Chinese emperor:

1405-07	Cheng Ho leads the fleet to Champa, Java, Sumatra, Ceylon, and Calicut.
1407-09	Admiral Ho's fleet under other leaders travels to Siam (Thailand) and Cochin (India).
1409-11	Ho again takes personal command, sailing to the East Indies, Quilan, and Ceylon.
1418-19	Ho guides his fleet to Java, Ryukyu, Brunei, and Aden.
1421-22	Ho again visits Java, Ryukyu, Brunei, and Aden.
1431-33	The admiral leads 200 ships and 27,550 men to Java, the Nicobar Islands, Mecca, and East Africa.

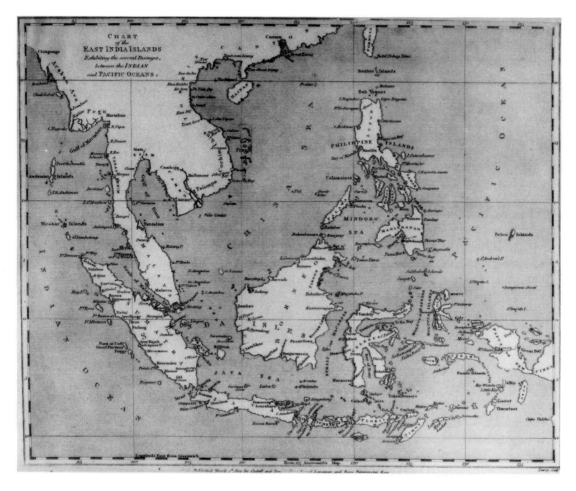

▲ Chart of the East India Islands; during his lifetime, Cheng Ho completed seven voyages that came to represent a unique period in world history.

exploration put an end to such expeditions. The succeeding Ch'ing dynasty's neglect of sea power left the Indian Ocean open—first to Arab traders who regained the spice lanes and later to aggressive European efforts to colonize Asia.

For More Information

Bloodworth, Dennis. *The Chinese Looking Glass*. Rev. ed. New York: Farrar, Strauss, 1980.

Li, Dun J. *The Civilization of China*. New York: Charles Scribner's Sons, 1975.

Mirsky, Jeanette. *The Great Chinese Travelers.* New York: Random House, 1964.

Yap, Yong, and Arthur Cotterell. *Chinese Civilization: From the Ming Revival to Chairman Mao.* New York: St. Martin's, 1977.

Vasco da Gama

c. 1460-1524

Personal Background

Early environment. Vasco da Gama was born in the seaport of Sines on the Alentejo coast of Portugal, where his father, Estevao da Gama, presided as civil governor. The family claimed a long history of nobility, tracing their roots back to late thirteenth-century Portuguese nobleman Alvaro da Gama.

Vasco da Gama was probably born in 1460, the year Henry the Navigator, the great Portuguese prince known for his love of science and exploration, had died. Henry strove to make Portugal a major world explorer; each year he outfitted two or three ships to travel along the African coast. Da Gama's father, who had trained at the royal nautical academy, led several of these expeditions to Africa.

In the family tradition, the younger da Gama was destined for a career at sea, but his early experience was with the military. While still a young man, he fought in Portugal's war with the Spanish kingdom of Castile. Later, he turned to the sea and established a reputation as an excellent navigator and crew manager. Very little is known about the dashing da Gama's early life, except that as many as four kings wanted him in their service. By the age of twenty-five he had been chosen to a high rank in the community as Grand Master of the Order of Christ. The youthful navigator had already gained a reputation as a strong, cool-headed ship's officer.

▲ **Vasco da Gama**

Event: Discovering a sea route to India.

Role: Vasco da Gama led the first Portuguese expedition to India and established a Portuguese trade center at Calicut on the southwest coast.

Participation:
Discovering a Sea Route to India

A passage to India. By the time da Gama was ready to direct ships, a great deal of exploring had already been done along the coast of Africa. Prince Henry eagerly supported the early Portuguese sea exploration, sponsoring voyages to the Canary islands, the Azores, and down the coast of Africa. By the time of Henry's death (and da Gama's birth), the west coast of Africa had been well charted by Portuguese sailors.

Bartolomeu Dias had earlier dispelled the notion that sailors traveling south would eventually slide off the edge of the earth. Driven by a fierce and freezing storm, he rounded the Cape of Good Hope (near Africa's southern tip) in 1487, landing at Mossel Bay. Dias sent back the message that there was really no obstacle to circling Africa and finding India. His expedition opened up the possibility of an eastern sea route to India; establishment of permanent trade with the East promised fabulous wealth if it could be accomplished.

Boundary dilemma. When Dias returned, Italian-born explorer Christopher Columbus was in Lisbon trying to secure support from King John of Portugal for his own voyage westward. Dias's cape-circling discovery, however, had worn away support for a search for a western route. Disappointed, Columbus was forced to turn to Ferdinand and Isabella of Spain for financial backing.

After discovering the Americas in 1492, Columbus personally delivered news of his New World adventures to King John. The Portuguese monarch immediately wanted to claim these lands and raced to assemble a fleet of ships. Ferdinand and Isabella of Spain responded by readying warships and petitioning Rome for exclusive rights to the recently discovered territories. The pope gave Spain all the lands opposite a line drawn one hundred leagues west of the Cape Verde islands, located off the west coast of Africa.

King John found this agreement unacceptable. War was avoided only when the pope, after a year of tense negotiations, arranged the Treaty of Tordesillas in June 1494. That agreement

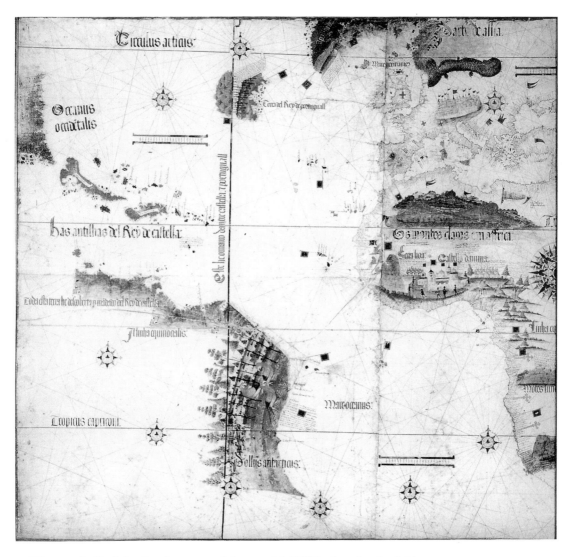

▲ **Western half of the Cantino map of the world, 1502, showing (at left) the Tordesillas Treaty demarcation line of 1494 that divided the undiscovered world between Spain and Portugal.**

established a new line 370 leagues west of the islands. Lands east of the boundary belonged to Portugal; the west was willed to Spain.

A new expedition. In the early 1490s King John sent several explorers to find an easy land route to the East. One such explorer, Pedro de Corvilhan, discovered the port of Sofala. Located about a hundred miles north of the Cape of Good Hope on the African coast, this harbor served as an important post on Arabian trade routes. Corvilhan told the king, "Anyone who will persist, is sure to sail around the southernmost point of Africa and can then easily make his way up the eastern shore and across the gulf to India" (Corvilhan in Horne, p. 139). The report convinced King John that a new path to India was possible. With profits on his mind, he began preparing ships for a voyage around the cape. But the monarch's health was failing; King John of Portugal died in October 1495.

Manuel I, nicknamed "the Fortunate," succeeded John to the throne of Portugal. The twenty-six-year-old king quickly moved to carry out what his father had planned. Within two months of his coronation, he presented a proposal for a new expedition to the East. Despite opposition from powerful Muslim merchants, the king persisted in his expensive undertaking. The ships were gathered and stocked to make the trip.

The ideal leader. Several historical accounts indicate da Gama's father was the original choice for the mission; his oldest brother may have turned it down as well. Legend has it that King Manuel noticed Vasco da Gama crossing the royal courtyard one day and apparently chose him as commander on a whim. Da Gama was widely known for his fiery temper, capable leadership, and confidence when dealing with sultans (Muslim kings), sailors, and savages. Diplomatic but firm, he possessed a broad vision and unquestionable authority.

Two years of preparation went into the building of da Gama's ships. Each one carried enough food for three years and was outfit-

---

Specialized Sailors, Custom Caravels

By modern standards, da Gama's four ships seem very small. The largest carried 120 tons; the other three were less than 100 feet long and carried less than 100 tons. Dias oversaw the ships' construction and built them according to his own plans, making modifications based on his own experiences in Africa. The *San Gabriel* and *San Rafael* were armed with a total of twenty large guns and several "bombards," a type of cannon that fired stone shot and was often used for signaling as well as defensive purposes. From wooden "castles" on the bow and stern, the crew could fight off enemy attempts to board the ship. Da Gama insisted the 170-person crew learn basic carpentry, caulking, and rope-making. A dozen convicts on board, who were serving death sentences, were used in dangerous situations.

ted with stone pillars, which were deposited at important locations along the route. (It was Portuguese custom to erect pillars wherever a ship landed, claiming the land for Portugal.) Diego Dias, a younger brother of Bartolomeu, went along as a private secretary. Another crew member, Martin Alonso—who had been held captive in the Congo—went along as a Bantu interpreter. According to the *Roteiro,* the main account of the voyage, da Gama's ships were separated by a dense fog. They are believed to have regrouped in the Cape Verde islands on July 26, 1497, and remained there until August 3, taking on water, wood, and fresh food.

Into the open ocean. From the islands in the Atlantic, da Gama plotted a course never before tried. Attempting to avoid the perilous African coastal currents, he sailed southwest into the open ocean, crossing the calms at their narrowest point and taking advantage of the prevailing winds. His wide semicircular course also allowed a survey of the western waters of the Atlantic given to Portugal under the Treaty of Tordesillas. The explorers remained at sea for ninety-six days in cramped quarters. Supplies had to be rationed, and the lack of fresh food resulted in severe illness. The crew's problems increased as they neared the southern tip of Africa and encountered icy storms caused by Antarctic ocean currents.

Trials and errors. After such a long time at sea, da Gama sighted land in November. The *Roteiro* entry reads: "We then drew near to each other, and having put on our gala clothes, we saluted the Captain Major by firing our bombards, and dressed the ships with flags and standards" (Stefannson, p. 163). They docked at St. Helena Bay to prepare for the next phase of the expedition. There the ships underwent minor repairs and were restocked with water, food, and fuel.

During their stay at St. Helena, da Gama and his crew were visited by Hottentots, described as "tawny colored natives" of southern Africa. One of the sailors is thought to have offended the Hottentot people while touring the local village. Da Gama was wounded while helping his shipmate to safety. The explorers' oversight is made clear in the *Roteiro:* "All this happened because we looked upon these people as men of little spirit, quite incapable of

17

violence, and had therefore landed without first arming ourselves" (Stefannson, p. 165). Da Gama would not repeat this mistake.

Cautious contact. Having left St. Helena after an eight-day stay, the ships rounded the Cape of Good Hope on November 22, 1497. They traveled up the eastern coast of Africa for a short distance and met the inhabitants of Mossel Bay. For thirteen days the Europeans remained there, trading and celebrating with the natives while repairing their ships. This time da Gama was prepared when peaceful trading deteriorated to discord. An alleged misunderstanding over the trading of bracelets for an ox caused da Gama to suspect some treachery. The men pulled away in their longboats and landed downshore, armed with lances and crossbows and armored with breastplates. Two bombards were fired, causing the native people to retreat.

The expedition then continued up the coast and on December 16 passed the furthest point attained by Dias on an earlier journey. Da Gama's crew members—like Dias's—rebelled over the prospect of crossing the Indian Ocean. But da Gama succeeded in suppressing the mutiny. In mid-January he reached the Quelimane River and dubbed it the *Rio dos Bons Sinaes* ("River of Good Omens"), since it signified a return to civilization.

Mozambique, Mombasa, and Malindi. Upon reaching the southeast African land of Mozambique in the late winter of 1498, da Gama found Arab ships laden with spices, gold, and precious stones. The inhabitants were not impressed by the size, or even the strangeness, of the Portuguese ships and assumed the unusual vessels came from some distant Muslim kingdom. Local officials went aboard to greet the newcomers, but their attitudes towards the Portuguese changed abruptly when da Gama revealed his religion and his mission.

Early April found the fleet anchored outside Mombasa, in present-day Kenya. Once again, da Gama explained the nature of his expedition and met with violent opposition. He and his crew easily staved off an armed boarding party from the city. During the struggle, Mozambican pilots leapt overboard. The fleet of ships was forced to continue onward without a reliable guide.

Da Gama's situation began to improve as he sailed northward. Approaching Malindi, he encountered a small boat offshore and entrusted the Muslims with a message for the local leader: he wished to establish friendly relations and obtain a pilot. The sultan of Malindi thought that da Gama could be a valuable ally against his enemy in Mombasa, so he provided a pilot. Favorable monsoon winds carried da Gama to Calicut in southwest India in twenty-three days.

Once in Calicut, da Gama found it difficult to set up a trading post because Arab traders were already well established with the Hindu rulers. Since the Europeans posed a threat to their virtual monopoly on trade, the Arabs denounced them and pushed for their expulsion from the area. The Indian ruler, or *rajah,* was swayed by the Arabs' arguments and had some of the Portuguese, including da Gama, taken prisoner. Fighting broke out in the city and da Gama managed to make his escape, returning to his ships and setting sail. He was still intent on profit but, after Calicut, was able to engage in only very limited trade in the ports they frequented. By January 1499 just two of da Gama's ships remained and more than half of the original crew had died. After being away from Portugal for nearly three years, da Gama sailed homeward.

Da Gama on Civilization in Africa
"Two gentlemen of the country came to see us. They were very haughty and valued nothing that we gave them. One of them wore a *touca,* with a fringe embroidered in silk, and the other a cap of green satin. A young man in their company—so we understood from their signs—had come from a distant country and had already seen big ships like ours" (Stefannson, p. 173).

Aftermath

Second voyage. Da Gama, now "Admiral of the Indian Seas," was rewarded with an annual income and granted the town of Sines. His expedition had succeeded but the costs had been high; two ships destroyed and scores of sailors dead. Da Gama's second voyage is notable for its viciousness and violence. In 1502 he returned to India with fifteen ships. His fleet overtook a ship returning from Mecca and set it on fire, burning alive all those aboard except for twenty women and children. At Kilwa he forced the leader to pay tribute. And when he learned of the violent

deaths of Portuguese explorers in Calicut—they had settled there after landing in the region with Portuguese explorer Pedro Cabral—he bombarded the city, ignoring the local ruler's pleas for peace. He then sailed south along the Indian coast toward Cochin, intent, it seems, on doing as much damage to India as possible.

Abandoned and recalled. Earlier, in 1500, da Gama married Catherina de Ataíde. On his return to Portugal several years later, the couple settled in Sines. Da Gama was given the title "Dom," which is usually reserved only for kings. Still, for twenty years after his last voyage, da Gama had strained relations with the rulers of Portugal. During this period of forced retirement, Vasco and Catherina raised six sons.

By 1511 the Portuguese ruled the spice trade and replaced the Arabs as the leading merchants on the Indian Ocean. A series of rulers called viceroys were sent to manage Portuguese India, but by the early 1520s Portuguese interests in the East were virtually destroyed. In 1524 da Gama was called out of retirement to become viceroy of India. He proceeded to Calicut to restore order but died shortly after his arrival.

For More Information

Boorstin, Daniel J. *The Discoverers: A History of Man's Search to Know His World and Himself.* New York: Random House, 1983.

Boxer, Charles R. *The Portuguese Seaborne Empire: 1415-1825.* New York: Alfred A. Knopf, 1969.

Horne, Charles F. *Great Men and Famous Women.* Vol. 5. New York: Selmar Hess, 1894.

Stefannson, Villhjalmur, editor. *Great Adventurers and Explorations.* New York: Dial Press, 1947.

◄
A 1747 engraving of da Gama being received by the rajah at Calicut in 1498. Da Gama found it difficult to set up a trading post there because Arab traders were already well established with the Hindu rulers.

Jacques Cartier

1491-1557

Personal Background

Mystery man. Jacques Cartier was a distinguished French navigator, but little is known about his life. No authentic portrait of him exists, and the few details of his biography were compiled from church and court records. He was born in 1491 in the province of Brittany in the city of Saint-Malo, a famed fishing port known for its sailors. A leader in his church and community, he presided as a sponsor in twenty-seven baptisms. In April 1520 he is believed to have married Catherine des Granches. There is no record of his career before 1532. However, the bishop of Saint-Malo, who recommended him to the king, claimed that Cartier had already traveled to Brazil and Newfoundland. Some sources suggest he accompanied Italian explorer Giovanni da Verrazano on his exploits in 1524, but such claims may be untrue.

Historical background. France was a late entry into the race for westward expansion; by the sixteenth century, the North American continent was the domain of Italian explorers. The French did not consider it profitable to cross the North Atlantic until Venetian navigator John Cabot reported large schools of fish along the Newfoundland coast, just east of Canada. Boats were then launched from Brittany and Normandy, and fisheries were established on the islands near Newfoundland. The northern fishermen brought knowledge of the region's waters, and France turned north to find a water route to trade in the East. Jacques

▲ **Jacques Cartier**

Event: French exploration of North America.

Role: A careful mapmaker and competent captain, Jacques Cartier was the first European to navigate and map the Gulf of St. Lawrence.

Cartier was chosen to lead the first expedition seeking a passage to Cathay (or China).

Participation:
Exploring the Gulf of St. Lawrence

Cartier left Saint-Malo on April 20, 1534, with two ships and sixty-one men. Sailing in good weather along the latitude of his home port, they made the crossing in only twenty days and arrived too early on the Newfoundland coast; ice still blocked their passage, and the ships were forced to wait for the thaw in a sheltered port. The region left a distinct impression on Cartier: "For in all the North Island I did not see a cart load of good earth ... and on the island of White Sand [Blanc Sablon] there is nothing else but moss and small thorns scattered here and there, withered and dry" (Cartier in Robinson, p. 357).

Cartier headed for the island of Brest to replenish his supplies of water and wood. On the way he met a fishing boat from La Rochelle that had lost its bearings and was able to set it back on course. His familiarity with the area has been taken as further evidence that he had been there before.

Paradise found. On June 15 Cartier began a careful exploration of the coastline, investigating every opening inland, carefully charting his course, taking soundings (measurements of depth), and recording his observations. The vast natural resources were of great interest to Cartier; he noted schools of salmon, mackerel, tuna, sturgeon, and cod; forests of cedars, yews, pines, elms, white ash, and willow; and wild wine grapes. He continued:

> It is hotter here than Spain, and the country is the fairest to be found, even if it be sandy. In every place it has trees or wild corn with an ear like rye, and small peas as thick as if they had been sown and plowed over, and red and white gooseberries, strawberries, blackberries, white and red roses and many other flowers of sweet smell. (Cartier in Lamb, p. 146)

Newfoundland. Despite Cartier's persistent search, the passage inland remained hidden in a maze of false bays and rivers that grew increasingly narrow. In late June he sighted Prince

Edward Island, mistaking it for part of the mainland; on July 3 he reached Chaleur Bay. With each dead end, he grew more and more disappointed.

On July 14, Cartier landed at Gaspé, where he found a great number of Iroquois on shore for their annual fishing excursion. The Iroquois people were an important power in the St. Lawrence River valley at the time. Nevertheless, the Cartier expedition erected a huge cross at Penouille Point, marking France's claim to the land. The meaning was clear to Donnacona, leader of the Iroquois, who approached Cartier's ship in protest, accompanied by three of his sons and his brother: "There he made a long oration unto us, showing us the cross we had set up, and making a cross with two fingers; then did he show us all the country about us, as if he would say that all was his" (Cartier in Robinson, p. 360).

The diplomatic Cartier assured the Indians that he and his crew meant no harm. He distributed gifts of clothing, red caps, knives, and copper necklaces to the chief's family and obtained permission to take two of the chief's sons, Domagaya and Taignoagny, to France, with a promise to return them the following year bearing iron wares and other goods.

Cartier departed in late July and steered eastward. Noting that the coast curved off towards the southwest, Cartier believed he had finally found the passage he sought. He had reached the mouth of the St. Lawrence River but was unable to explore further. Bad weather reportedly forced him to withdraw on August 15.

Second voyage. Cartier returned to Saint-Malo to report his findings to King Francis I. He related his discovery of an inland sea in a fertile new land and within a month was given another commission and a greater sum of money. On this second voyage, he commanded three ships, the *Grande Hermine,* the *Petite Hermine,* and the *Emerillion,* and 110 men, including chief Donnacona's two sons. Cartier left Saint-Malo on May 19, 1535. This time the Atlantic crossing took fifty days because of severe storms. Still the navigator immediately picked up where he had left off. The Indians assured him that there was, indeed, a great river to the west that flowed in ever-narrowing passage until it reached the middle of Canada. The territory's fresh water

▲ Illustration by C. W. Jefferys of Cartier and his men meeting with the Huron and Iroquois of the St. Lawrence River in 1535.

streams were said to stretch so far north and west that no one had ever explored them.

Historical evidence indicates that Donnacona wanted to escape the hold that the chief of Hochelaga (a village in the region that is now Montreal) had over all the Iroquois of the valley. He sought to secure for his tribe the sole future rights to trade with the French, trying first to detain Cartier with gifts, and when this failed, with a display of witchcraft. Cartier left the village on September 19 without interpreters. He stopped at Achelacy and formed an alliance with the local chieftain. Leaving his ship at anchor at Lake Angouleme, he continued on in the longboats with thirty of his men.

Cartier and his crew met a joyous reception in Hochelaga on October 2. From the top of a hill he called *Mont Royal,* Cartier saw the sweeping panorama of the North American continent, with the great river—which he later named the St. Lawrence—trailing off in the distant southwest. He questioned the Indians about what lay beyond and learned of more difficult rapids upriver and of the rich northern land of Saguenay, a powerful—but imaginary—Indian nation.

Winter and disease. Cartier returned to the Iroquois headquarters of Stadacona but was unprepared for the severe winter season. Snow fell four feet deep, and from mid-November to mid-April the ships were locked in ice. "We were held in ice two fathoms thick, and snow [rose] above the rails of our ships. All our drinks were frozen, and the ice thickened below hatches as well as above" (Cartier in Lamb, p. 155). Around the same time, relations with the Iroquois began to weaken. The Indians still traded Cartier meat and parched maize, but at high prices. The poor diet brought on scurvy, claiming the lives of twenty-five members of the crew in a few months. Cartier's intelligence and skill proved useless against the disease, and in desperation he led a procession to pray before an image of the Virgin Mary for relief. Soon afterward, he is said to have learned of an Indian remedy made from the bark and leaves of the *anneda* (white cedar). The folk medicine quickly cured the remaining crew.

In early May, Cartier left North America with about ten Iroquois, including four children and Donnacona. Fourteen months after their departure from France, the expedition arrived back home. To King Francis, the second voyage seemed even better than the first: Cartier returned with knowledge of a river that led far into the new lands. In addition, he had made new contacts and had become familiar with the territory's available resources.

Third voyage. The king commissioned a third voyage in 1541. Cartier was given the title "captain general," along with broad authority to proceed as far as Saguenay and live with the natives if need be. Cartier began preparations immediately, assembling a diverse and capable crew.

But King Francis later granted a new commission to explorer Jean-Francois de la Rocque de Roberval to claim the

▲ The disembarkation of Cartier and French settlers in Canada in 1542 on his third voyage; Cartier was given the authority to live with the natives if need be.

land for France and establish a base in New France, as the St. Lawrence region was called. Although Cartier remained in charge of navigation and discovery at sea, Roberval—the real leader—was given authority over the entire expedition.

Cartier set sail in the spring of 1541 with fifteen hundred men and five ships. The voyagers returned to Stadacona on August 23. They informed the Iroquois nation that their leader, Donnacona, had died; the other tribal leaders had settled in France and did not want to return home.

Cartier began the construction of two forts, then sailed to meet the chieftain of Achelacy. In an unprecedented move, he left two European boys there to be schooled in the local language. Cartier wanted to survey the rapids so he could cross them the following spring, but accounts of his voyage become sketchy during this time. Soon after departing for France, he is believed to have encountered Roberval and his fleet at St. John's. Roberval ordered him to turn back, but Cartier defied his orders and sailed away in the dead of night.

Aftermath

Although Cartier was not punished for his disobedience, he never commanded another expedition. The "diamonds" and "gold" he gave to King Francis turned out to be a worthless collection of quartz and iron pyrite ("fool's gold"). Cartier appeared before a tribunal in the spring of 1544 to sort out his debts from Roberval's and proved that he had used the king's money in good faith. He was repaid about nine thousand livres.

Cartier spent most of his later years making business deals and maintaining his estate of Limoilou. The documents of this period refer to him as a *noble homme* (or "nobleman"). He died on September 1, 1557, at the age of sixty-six.

Failed colonies in Canada. Roberval continued up the St. Lawrence and rebuilt Cartier's abandoned settlement. During the harsh winter, he resorted to drastic disciplinary measures—including the execution of fifty people—to maintain order among the colonists. Roberval's exploration came to an abrupt end in June 1543, when his boat was wrecked. He headed for France in September.

After Francis I's death in 1574, his son Henry II showed no interest in America. A period of religious wars in Europe and dissension within the Catholic Church postponed further exploration of the New World. For more than fifty years, no other French explorer set foot on Canadian shores.

For More Information

Barclay, Elizabeth. *Worlds without End.* Garden City, New York: Doubleday, 1956.

Lamb, Harold. *New Found World.* Garden City, New York: Doubleday, 1955.

Pendergast, James F., and Bruce G. Trigger. *Cartier's Hochelaga and the Dawson Site.* Toronto: University of Toronto Press, 1972.

Robinson, Conway. *Early Voyages to America.* Richmond, Virginia: Shepherd & Colin, 1848.

Religious Reform

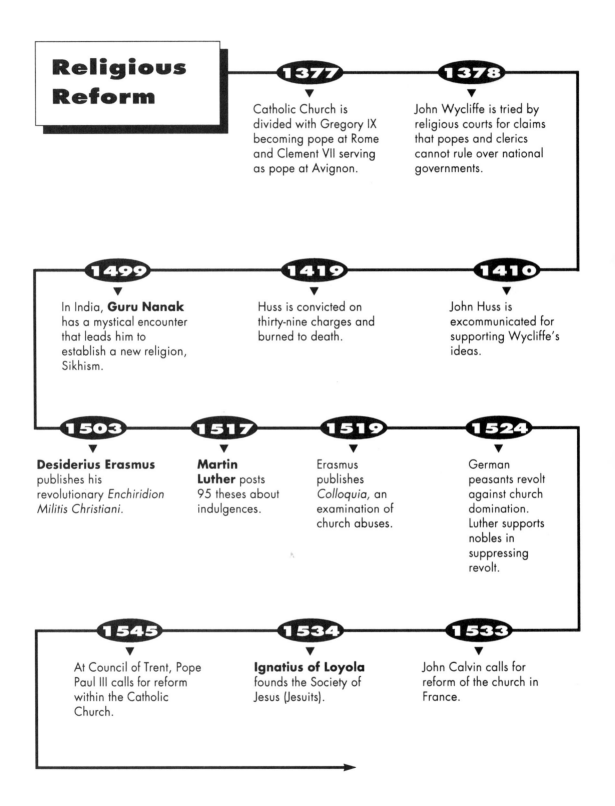

1377
Catholic Church is divided with Gregory IX becoming pope at Rome and Clement VII serving as pope at Avignon.

1378
John Wycliffe is tried by religious courts for claims that popes and clerics cannot rule over national governments.

1499
In India, **Guru Nanak** has a mystical encounter that leads him to establish a new religion, Sikhism.

1419
Huss is convicted on thirty-nine charges and burned to death.

1410
John Huss is excommunicated for supporting Wycliffe's ideas.

1503
Desiderius Erasmus publishes his revolutionary *Enchiridion Militis Christiani*.

1517
Martin Luther posts 95 theses about indulgences.

1519
Erasmus publishes *Colloquia*, an examination of church abuses.

1524
German peasants revolt against church domination. Luther supports nobles in suppressing revolt.

1545
At Council of Trent, Pope Paul III calls for reform within the Catholic Church.

1534
Ignatius of Loyola founds the Society of Jesus (Jesuits).

1533
John Calvin calls for reform of the church in France.

RELIGIOUS REFORM

Throughout the long period known as the Middle Ages (spanning a thousand years between 500 and 1500), Europe was dominated by strong religious and government bodies that worked together in close alliance. Most of the people of Europe were united in a single religion, Roman Catholicism. The good of church and state was paramount, and popes and kings exercised joint authority over the population. Through the years, nobles and clergymen grew wealthy at the expense of peasants. However, kings and popes occasionally broke the bonds between them to squabble over their respective rights. At times, the church ruled over emperors; at other times, kings chose and controlled the church leaders.

Academic learning was not widely encouraged in the Middle Ages. The growth of knowledge was limited to attempts to understand the scriptures and the stars. European scholars showed a growing interest in forecasting the future based on positions of celestial bodies.

Division of the church. Gradually, though, an intellectual awakening spread throughout Europe. As nobles and priests grew more corrupt and thoughtless, the common people began to challenge their control. Divisions between royalty and church leaders reached new heights in the early 1300s. In France, for example, King Philip IV tried to rid himself of the competition of Pope Boniface VIII. When Boniface died, Philip chose his own pope, Clement V, and moved the seat of the Catholic Church from Rome to France. Romans then chose their own pope. After 1377 the Catholic Church had no unified, centralized government. The division prompted some Catholic clergymen to look for ways to revive the old ideals of the church and rid it of corruption.

Priestly objections. Desiderius Erasmus, John Wycliffe, and John Huss were Catholic priests who, at different times, pushed for reform in the church. Erasmus wrote scathing essays about the misdeeds of priests and monks, while Wycliffe took exception mostly to one church practice—the granting of "indulgences" (the forgiving of sins). Confession of sins and consequent forgiveness had long been a part of Catholic belief. Over hundreds of years, confession to a priest had become a requirement for church members, but the forgiveness had become subject to the amount of money a confessor could contribute to the church.

Pope Leo X's enthusiasm for rebuilding the famous St. Peter's Cathedral in Rome led him to accept one priest's idea of charging increased fees for indulgences. This angered a German priest named **Martin Luther.** In 1517 Luther posted 95 theses (positions about indulgences) on the door of his church, challenging anyone to debate them. He was called to appear before a church court in Rome but never showed up; only the intervention of royal friends kept him from the fate of an earlier protester, John Huss. Huss had protested religious misdealings a century before and was burned to death for his convictions. Luther's actions triggered a peasant revolt in Europe—and with it the realization of reformed church ideas. Protestantism—named for the "protest" against the questionable practices of the Catholic Church—became an alternative to Catholicism.

Internal and external reform. Not all the clergy, however, had given up on the hope of renewal within the Catholic Church. One priest who believed in the possibility of reformed Catholicism was **Ignatius of Loyola.** He founded a new order, the Society of Jesus (or Jesuits), for that purpose. Jesuits organized under the old principles of the church, including loyalty to papal authority.

During the Reformation, the Catholic Church underwent significant changes. At the same time, new churches arose under the mantle of Protestantism. These Protestant churches abandoned the Catholic idea of salvation through priests and popes, teaching instead that salvation could be achieved through an individual worshipper's relationship with God. The idea grew, spawning several new religious movements and threatening to weaken Catholicism. Recognizing the danger and its causes, Pope Paul III called the Council of Trent in 1545 to begin massive reforms within the Catholic Church.

Religious reform in Asia. Late in the fifteenth century in India, a shepherd and government official named **Guru Nanak** became concerned over fragmentation and division within the Hindu and Islamic religions in his country. Nanak set out to reform religious practices. He spoke out against the suppression of human beings in the caste system (a hierarchical social system) and taught about the importance of each individual's obligation in leading a virtuous life. Nanak gained strong followers who united in a new religion, the religion of the Sikhs, after his death.

Desiderius Erasmus

c. 1466-1536

Personal Background

Humble beginnings of a great scholar. Desiderius Erasmus was born in about 1466 in Gouda, near Rotterdam, then a small country-town in Holland. He and his older brother, Peter, were both born out of wedlock to the same parents. Erasmus's father, Gerard (Rogerius Gerardus), was separated from his children and their mother, Margaret, by his own meddling family. Gerard later became a priest.

Orphaned by the plague. Erasmus and his brother were raised by their mother in a religious atmosphere. Erasmus served as a singer in the cathedral at Utrecht until he was nine years old. The two boys were then sent to a school in Deventer. It was at this school that Erasmus began to show his brilliance and his love for learning.

Margaret died during an outbreak of the plague in about 1479. The brothers were placed in the care of their father, who was also killed by the plague a few weeks later. A despicable uncle became the guardian of the orphaned teenagers; he quickly sent them off to a monastery—and spent all of the money left to them by their father.

Erasmus clashed with authorities at the monastery. He felt that the monks were immoral and their rules were unfair. His main goal was to become a scholar, not a member of the clergy.

▲ Desiderius Erasmus

Event: The Reformation of the Catholic Church.

Role: Desiderius Erasmus was the leading expert on Latin and Greek literature in the late fifteenth and early sixteenth centuries. He is best known for his translations of the Christian scriptures and his criticism of the Catholic Church, which encouraged religious reform.

Under pressure from family and church leaders, Erasmus's brother was ordained a monk. Because Erasmus refused to follow his brother's example, he was disowned by his uncle and forced to leave the monastery. Unable to afford a university education, he joined Steyn, a more liberal Augustinian monastery, and studied Latin literature. Eventually, he too was ordained.

Leaving monastic life. After living at Steyn for a few years, Erasmus became an expert in Latin literature. The Bishop of Cambrais, impressed with the young monk's wealth of knowledge, invited him to become a member of his court and travel with him to Rome. Although the trip to Rome never materialized, the bishop did give Erasmus enough money to enroll in a university in Paris, France.

A scholar at last. Erasmus lived a very modest life in a Paris boarding house and attended the Collège Montaigu. After working for a while as a part-time professor and occasional beggar, he landed a job as a private tutor to English students. One of the Englishmen, Lord Mountjoy, was so impressed with Erasmus's teaching abilities that he gave him a small pension for life. The scholar's reputation grew, and he was soon able to save up enough money to travel to places of interest to him.

Travel in search of knowledge. Throughout his life, Erasmus made several countries his home. He lived in Holland, France, England, and Switzerland—usually not for more than two or three years at a time. He did not consider himself a citizen of any one country, but rather a citizen of the world. Scholars indicate that Erasmus may not have even known his native language, Dutch. He loved Latin and Greek so much that he spoke and wrote in both almost exclusively.

Participation: Erasmus's Religious Critiques

Life in England. In the late 1490s, after his stay in Paris, Erasmus moved with his friends to England. He stayed only a short time before returning to France and then traveling to Italy. Around the same time, he asked to be relieved of his priestly commitment, and the pope agreed. Soon thereafter he returned to England, where he found a community of people who enjoyed Latin

▲ Sixteenth-century engraving of Erasmus in conversation with friends at Oxford around 1500; in England Erasmus found a community of people who enjoyed Latin and Greek literature as much as he did.

and Greek literature as much as he did. In this stimulating atmosphere, Erasmus began to criticize alleged corruption and abuses within the ranks of the Catholic Church.

Reasons for reform. Erasmus's complaints about the monks and the practices of the church were not unfounded. By the 1400s the Catholic Church had become more like a political organization than a community of worship. For example, churches often raised money by selling pardons for sins (called "indulgences"); a follower was granted forgiveness for sins if he or she paid a certain amount to the priest. As disdain for such church practices continued to grow, Erasmus decided to retranslate original Greek Christian texts in order to show the true relationship between God and human beings.

Writings. Erasmus made this translation project his life's work. To supplement his income while mastering the Greek language, he wrote and published several books, including humorous satires, theological essays, and translations of Latin and Greek poetry. In one particular satirical volume, Erasmus poked fun at kings, princes, bishops, and popes. Beyond its humor, this work served as a powerful testament to the author's belief that no one should be a slave to the state or the church.

Erasmus considered religion the ultimate science, and he became a specialist in the field of theology. His first religious book, a revolutionary volume titled *Enchiridion Militis Christiani,* was published in 1503. In it Erasmus describes the difference between attending church and having true faith. He believed that people did not have to attend services to have a spiritual relationship with God.

Erasmus became a professor of divinity and Greek at Cambridge University in England and completed his new Latin translation of the Greek New Testament. He also wrote extensively on the damaging effects of mysticism and ritual in the church. In 1519 he published his masterpiece, *Colloquia,* an examination of church abuses.

Erasmus and the Plague

Part of the reason that Erasmus kept moving from place to place was to avoid the plague and other illnesses. When his friend Faustus Andrelinus accused him of being a coward for leaving Paris because of an outbreak of the plague, Erasmus replied:

> In this condition of things I wouldn't hesitate to fly, not merely to Orléans, but to Cadiz or to the farthest of the far Orkneys; not because I am a timid person or of less than manly courage, but because I really do fear—not to die, for we are all born to die—but to die by my own fault. (Erasmus in Emerton, p. 92)

Aftermath

A wealth of inspiration. Through his interpretation of the Latin and Greek Christian texts, Erasmus made a purer form of religion available to the population. His work provided a basis for important religious reformers who would follow him. Men like Martin Luther were inspired by his words and took action as a result.

But Erasmus himself never actually became a forceful agitator for reform. Martin Luther sent Erasmus a letter in 1519, while the Reformation was taking place, asking him to take a more active role in rebuilding the church. He replied that he admired Luther's ideals but did not agree with his practice of using force to make change. Erasmus preferred to think that reform would come about naturally as individuals made the same discoveries about religion that he had made.

Reformers sought to restore the church to its more traditional and purer structure. Erasmus, however, did not see the need for any such structure. In fact, he was somewhat troubled by the nature of the Reformation because he apparently did not believe that people needed any form of organized religion to maintain a relationship with God. He became increasingly disturbed by the forceful methods of change employed by the leaders of the Reformation and clung to his belief in passive resistance until he died.

> ### A Scholar's Humor
>
> It is clear from his works that Erasmus possessed a great sense of humor. For example, he hated fish—a food that Catholics traditionally ate on Fridays. Because of this, he once announced that his heart was Catholic, but his stomach was Lutheran.

Erasmus's inevitable death. By the late 1520s Erasmus's health was declining and he was beginning to lose faith in humanity. Over the next decade, he is said to have looked forward to death, viewing it as relief from the turmoil in life. In 1535 he decided to return to Holland to live out the rest of his days. He died there the next year.

Renaissance man. Erasmus contributed to the spiritual aspect of the Renaissance. While artists were reinterpreting newly discovered classical models and scientists were expanding the boundaries of human thought, Erasmus rediscovered the early Christian scriptures and brought them to the world's attention. He is credited with raising the study of religion to a higher level and inspiring the reformation of the Christian Church.

For More Information

Emerton, Ephraim. *Desiderius Erasmus of Rotterdam.* New York: Putnam, 1899.

Huizinga, Johan. *Erasmus and the Age of Reformation.* New York: Harper, 1957.

Wright, Esmond, editor. *History of the World.* Volume 1 of *The Awakening of Man.* New York: Crown, 1985.

Guru Nanak

c. 1469-1539

Personal Background

Birth and early life. Nanak was born around 1469 in the village of Talwandi Rai Bhol (now Nankana), in present-day Pakistan. From an early age, he displayed an unusual curiosity about the spiritual nature of human beings. By the time he was five he was asking questions about the purpose of life. He was tutored in language and mathematics at the age of seven and, two years later, was sent to a renowned Muslim teacher to learn Persian and Arabic.

As a young student, Nanak was preoccupied with questions about religion. Though born a Hindu, he was later influenced by the Islamic faith. He met with holy men to discuss the mysteries of spirituality and spent time by himself pondering what he learned.

At the age of twelve, according to Indian custom, Nanak was married. He did not live with his wife, Sulakhni, until seven years later. A few years after that, the couple had two sons, Sri Chand and Lakhmi Das. For a time, Nanak's obsession with religion distracted him from pursuing a practical occupation. In order to provide for his family, though, he eventually settled on a job as an accountant for the sultan (king) of Delhi.

The encounter that changed his life. At the turn of the sixteenth century, while working for the sultan, Nanak moved to

▲ One of the Indian gods, Shiva; Nanak's new religion proposed one god and one unified society as an alternative for both Hindus and Muslims.

Event: Founding of the Sikhs.

Role: Guru Nanak brought about religious reformation in India. He was the founding father of Sikhism, a religion that unified the people of northwestern India and served as the basis for a major political movement.

his sister's home in Sultanpur. There he met a Muslim minstrel, and together they organized a group that met in the evenings to sing hymns. After a particularly long night of singing, Nanak had a mystical encounter at a nearby river. He is said to have heard God speak to him. His own account relates God's message:

> Nanak, I am with thee. Through thee will my name be magnified. Whosoever follows thee, him I will save. Go into the world to pray and teach mankind how to pray. Be not sullied by the ways of the world. Let your life be one of praise of the Word, charity, ablution [or washing, as part of a religious rite], service, and prayer. Nanak, I give thee My pledge. Let this be thy life's mission (Singh, p. 31).

At this time, most people in India were polytheistic—they believed in several gods. Nanak's experience led him to believe in one supreme God. At the age of thirty, he became the supreme "guru" (teacher) of God's word.

Nanak disappeared for three days after his encounter. The townspeople assumed that he had drowned in the river. On the fourth day, Nanak returned to the town and gave away all of his possessions, including his clothes, keeping nothing but a loin cloth. The next day, he went to stay with Muslim monks and later spoke the words: "There is no Hindu, there is no Mussalman" (Nanak in Singh, p. 33). With that, Guru Nanak began a new life for himself that would soon alter the religious lives of many Indians.

Participation: Founding the Sikh Religion

Motivated by the poor state of religious and political affairs in India at the time, Nanak set out to spread the word about God. He felt that the Hindu and Muslim faiths had become corrupt and wanted to offer a more pure, simple, and accessible faith to the Indian people. "The age is like a knife. Kings are butchers. Religion hath taken wings and flown," he said (Singh, p. 29).

Nanak journeyed primarily through the Punjab region of northwest India. Bordered by mountains to the north and by the desert to the south, this area was often subject to invasion by for-

▲ Though he journeyed primarily through the Punjab region of northwest India, Nanak made a pilgrimage to the Muslim holy city of Mecca.

eign armies. The multicultural region was eventually united under one new language, Punjabi, although the people remained divided by politics and religion.

Chief guru. Nanak continued his travels throughout India and out of the country as far west as Baghdad. He also made pilgrimages to the Muslim holy cities of Mecca and Medina and later put his beliefs into writing in the *Adi-Granth*. When his initial touring was finished, he settled down with his family in a township that he had built called Kartarpur, which means "the abode of the Creator." Nanak was now the chief guru of a new religion. His followers called themselves "Sikhs" (pronounced "seeks"), which means "disciples."

Guru Nanak was a gentle, courageous man who sought to unite all of Indian society into one religion and one social class. This was a real challenge in India, where the dominant religions—Islamic and Hindu—followed strict laws of social stratification. As he traveled, Nanak established places of worship for the Sikhs. He also founded community kitchens and dining areas so that people of different castes (restrictive Hindu social classes) could eat together. This was a revolutionary practice at a time when people believed that if a person from a lower caste passed over the place where food was being prepared, the food was rendered impure and unfit to eat.

Worship in Darkness

Guru Nanak used unconventional means to communicate his vision. He was a humorist, a poet, and a painter. His exceptional collections of verse on Sikhism helped to make him very popular. Many of his poems were put to music and became hymns. Nanak encouraged his followers to wake up hours before dawn so that they could sing these hymns under the stars. He believed that the dark morning hours were the best time for spiritual pursuits—and the time when people could feel closest to God.

Appeal of the new religion. Nanak's new religion proposed one God and one unified society as an alternative for both Hindus and Muslims. The guru used logic to show that the beliefs and rituals of other religions were not practical. On one occasion, he went to the Ganges River, where he saw several people offering water to the sun. (The holy men had promised them it would reach their ancestors in the land of the gods.) In a surprising move, Nanak began to offer water in a completely different direction, telling people if their water would make it all the way to their ancestors, his water would easily make it to his drought-inflicted farm. When the people considered how unlikely it was that Nanak's water would reach his farm, they realized how unlikely it was that their water would reach the land of the gods. According to the story, the listeners bowed at Nanak's feet and became disciples of his new religion.

Aftermath

Death and succession. When it came time for Nanak to select the next Sikh guru, he did not choose either of his sons. His elder son, Sri Chand, believed in a different religion; his younger son, Lakhmi Das, did not adhere to any specific religion. Left with no heir to the leadership of the Sikhs, Guru Nanak selected a man named Lehna, who had developed a following in his own right.

Lehna was noted for his extreme devotion and his gift for leadership. Nanak renamed him "Angad," meaning "of my own limb."

In September 1539 Guru Nanak died at his home in Kartarpur. Throughout his career as guru of the Sikhs, he tried to unite the Hindus and the Muslims. The first four gurus who succeeded him followed his policy of noninvolvement in civil affairs. However, the fifth guru, Arjun, took the side of a prince in a rebellion. After that, the Sikhs became more and more involved in government affairs until the new religion grew into a powerful political body. By the close of the twentieth century, more than three million residents of northern India followed the religion of the Sikhs.

Sikhism

Gurus are believed to guide Sikhs to salvation by instructing them on the ways of God and the avoidance of sin. The three commandments of the Sikhs are to work, to worship, and to give in charity. The five sins are lust, anger, greed, attachment, and pride.

For More Information

Naidis, Mark. *India: A Short Introductory History*. New York: Macmillan, 1966.

Riencourt, Amaury de. *The Soul of India*. New York: Harper, 1960.

Singh, Khushwant. *A History of the Sikhs*. Vol. 1: *1469-1839*. Princeton, New Jersey: Princeton University Press, 1963.

Ignatius of Loyola

1491-1556

Personal Background

Birth and early life. The youngest of thirteen children, Ignatius of Loyola was born Iñigo López de Recalde in 1491. His parents lived in the castle of Loyola in the kingdom of Castile, a Spanish territory where his father served as a soldier. Ignatius's mother died when he was a baby; because his father was often away fighting, the young boy was raised by a neighbor woman. She taught him about faith, devotion, and loyalty—qualities that he valued for the rest of his life.

As a teenager, Ignatius longed for the glamorous life of a soldier. His father lacked the money needed to provide him with military training and urged him to become a notary or a scrivener (a professional writer). Disappointed with his future prospects, Ignatius eagerly accepted an offer of a more exciting life with a nobleman named Juan Velasquez.

A gentleman of the court. Velasquez, a friend of Ignatius's father, invited Ignatius to live with him. Ignatius accepted and traveled over four hundred miles, probably on the back of a mule, to reach his destination. There he was schooled in the ways of the Spanish court, and in his free time he probably rode horses, practiced fencing, attended dances, gambled, and learned about weaponry.

▲ **Ignatius of Loyola**

Event: Founding the Jesuit Order.

Role: Ignatius of Loyola was a Spanish nobleman who, at the age of thirty, decided to devote himself to the service of Jesus Christ. In 1534 he created a new priestly order called the Society of Jesus to carry out the work of the church. He was canonized in 1622.

Charles V. Ignatius's adventurous life with Velasquez came to an abrupt end when King Ferdinand of Spain died in 1516. A German monarch named Charles V then rose to power in Spain. He soon filled the Spanish high offices with new officials, and Velasquez lost his place in the Spanish court. Ignatius, then about twenty-six years old, moved back to Loyola.

A soldier. Queen Isabella and King Ferdinand had been very popular with the Spanish people. Charles V's rule was less successful and sparked civil wars in the kingdom. Within a few years, Ignatius was called upon for the first time to go into battle. He had not been formally trained as a soldier, but the Duke of Najera took him on as a gentleman attendant. The duke and his troops were successful in the civil war, and Ignatius stayed on with the intention of being a career soldier. He was already establishing a reputation as a fierce warrior.

War with France. Soon after the civil wars quieted down, France invaded parts of Spain and its territories. Ignatius played a significant role in the battle at Pamplona in 1521. France seemed the likely winner of the conflict, but Ignatius urged the Spanish army to defend the town's fortress. During the battle, a bullet shattered the bones in Ignatius's right leg. Historical records indicate that immediately after he was hit, the Spanish soldiers surrendered to the French.

French doctors operated on Ignatius's leg and sent him back to Spain. During the journey, the bones began to heal incorrectly, so Spanish doctors later broke the leg again and reset it. However, parts of the bone overlapped during the healing process, causing his right leg to shorten and creating an unsightly bump that would certainly show in the tight stockings of an aristocrat. Anxious to have the defect corrected, Ignatius asked the doctors to remove the bump and lengthen his leg in yet another operation.

Recovery and discovery. While recovering from the painful surgery—there was no effective anesthetic at the time—Ignatius grew very ill. At one point, he was expected to die and was even given the last rights by a Catholic priest. The very next day, he began to recover. During his convalescence, he read two Catholic books: *The Life of Christ* and a volume on the lives of the saints called *The Flower of the Saints*. These two books changed his life.

For five months, while confined to his bed, Ignatius read the religious stories over and over again. From this point on, his thoughts about worldly pleasures left him unfulfilled. He decided to devote his life to the service of God.

Readying himself for the journey. When he felt well enough to walk, Ignatius embarked on a pilgrimage to Jerusalem. He was now thirty years old and walked with a limp. Abandoning his earlier lifestyle altogether, he planned to beg for food and shelter and rely on the support of his friends to see him through the journey.

His first destination was a monastery in Montserrat in northeastern Spain, where he studied Catholicism. Ignatius stayed there for almost all of 1522 and prepared his soul for the pilgrimage through a rigorous regimen of prayer, fasting, and confession of his sins. He ate only bread and water Monday through Saturday and prayed on his knees seven hours a day. Occasionally he believed that he saw visions of Mary, the baby Jesus, and other religious images. Eventually Ignatius came to terms with his sins. Vowing to lead a life of poverty and simplicity, he hung up his soldier's weapons, gave away his rich clothing, and went to a neighboring town to serve the sick and poor.

Ignatius and Desiderius Erasmus

Ignatius and Desiderius Erasmus were both very influential and well-respected religious reformers, but they were nothing alike. Ignatius was said to have been very humble, emotional, and strong. Erasmus, on the other hand, was very proud, intellectual, and frail. Ignatius once read Erasmus's popular book *Enchiridion Militis Christiani* (*The Christian Soldier's Manual*) and had a very strange reaction. As he read it, his devotion to God began to fade. The more he read, the weaker his devotion became. Ignatius was so disturbed by this that he threw the book aside. After this experience, he decided that those who followed him could only read pre-approved sections of Erasmus's work.

Participation: Founding the Jesuit Order

The pilgrimage. With nothing more than a robe made of sackcloth (a rough, coarse material), a rope sandal on his right foot, and a book of religious notes, Ignatius set off for Rome, then for Jerusalem. He believed that God would help him reach his destinations safely.

After arriving in Jerusalem, Ignatius went to a convent established by other friars. He was turned away by the friars, though, mainly because of the dangerous political turmoil brewing in the region during the sixteenth century. Deeply disappointed, Ignatius returned to Barcelona, Spain, to study Latin. He felt that higher education would enable him to better serve God.

A controversial religious figure. Ignatius quickly established himself as a wise and trusted religious counselor. But during this age of reformation in Europe, officials in the Catholic Church were very suspicious of people who stirred up controversy with new ideas about religion. Ignatius soon became the subject of an investigation by church authorities. They ruled that he would not be allowed to teach religion again until he had completed an additional three years of training.

On to Paris. Ignatius made his way to France to free himself from the church-imposed restrictions on his teaching. He made six close friends in Paris, and together they promised to dedicate themselves to spreading God's word. Even though Ignatius and his companions at first wanted only to work for the salvation of souls, by 1534 they were taking steps to form a new religious order called the Society of Jesus, or the Order of Jesuits. The seven men saw themselves as soldiers charged with carrying out the work of the church and sought to establish a permanent base in Jerusalem. But Ignatius's ongoing battles with ill health caused them to delay their plans for the move.

While recovering from a severe fever, Ignatius stayed in a town close to Loyola, the city of his birth. He preached four times a day, taught classes for children, and helped to pass laws banning gambling and adultery. In 1537 the Jesuits were reunited in Venice. They had increased their membership by four and were preparing to leave for Jerusalem. Pope Paul III in Rome financed the trip and gave permission for Ignatius and several other members of the group to be ordained. That summer, when he was forty-six years old, Ignatius took his vows on an island off the Dalmatian coast, just across the Adriatic Sea from Italy. He said his first mass on Christmas Day in 1538.

Ignatius of Loyola

Ignatius was known by his given name, Iñigo, until he was about fifty-five years old. Some historians feel that he took the name Ignatius of Loyola because it sounded more Latin or Greek. It is more likely that he changed his name as a tribute to Ignatius of Antioch, who had been thrown to the beasts in Rome as a martyr.

The friends never made their trip to the Holy Land. At the time, the people of Jerusalem were engaged in a long struggle against Turkish rule, and for two years the Turkish fleet did not allow anyone to enter the region. Ignatius and the rest of the group remained in Italy, preaching in various churches and working with the sick and dying in local hospitals. In 1539, armed with a strict constitution prepared by Ignatius, they petitioned the pope to allow the formation of a new Catholic order. The Society of Jesus, or Order of Jesuits, was approved the next year.

Aftermath

Writings. Ignatius designed a new educational method that became a model for Jesuit schools. He also wrote a book called *Spiritual Exercises,* which he used to maintain his pure devotion to God. The volume served as a guide for Jesuit life. By the mid-1550s the society had spread through Italy, Spain, and Portugal and reached as far as Japan, India, and Brazil.

Ignatius died in 1556 after suffering from stomach pains and fever—the troubles that had been with him since he was thirty. His condition was not diagnosed until after his death, when the surgeon found countless stones in his kidneys, lungs, liver, and portal vein. Despite the agony it must have caused him, he barely let it or anything else slow him down in his work to glorify God. Ignatius was beatified (proclaimed as blessed by the church) in 1609 and canonized (named a saint) in 1622.

For More Information

Brodrick, James. *Saint Ignatius Loyola: The Pilgrim Years.* New York: Farrar, Straus, 1956.

O'Callaghan, Joseph F. *The Autobiography of Ignatius Loyola, with Related Documents.* New York: Harper, 1974.

Martin Luther

1483-1546

Personal Background

Birth and early life. Martin Luther was born in 1483 at Eisleben, a German territory of the Holy Roman Empire. Shortly afterward, the family moved to Mansfeld, where his father, Hans Luder ("Luder" later became translated as "Luther") worked as a miner. Hans eventually became a business partner in several small copper mines. Over the years, he saved what money he could and planned to send Martin to law school.

Witches, superstitions, and religion. During the late fifteenth and early sixteenth centuries, superstitions flourished throughout Europe—even though the church was the center of society. People who lived in mining towns often blamed demons and evil spirits for mine-related accidents and deaths. Luther's parents were not particularly religious and apparently believed that one of their children had been killed by a witch. With a background such as this, Luther hardly seemed destined to play such an important role in the history of religion.

Education. Luther spent eight years at a strict grammar school and became fluent in Latin. At the age of thirteen, he moved to the city of Magdenburg and studied in a monastery school. While there, Luther joined a boys' choir that went door to door to sing for donations for the monastery. Music remained an important part of his life; he later learned how to the play the lute, a large stringed instrument, and wrote songs for the choir.

▲ Martin Luther

Event: Beginning the Protestant Reformation.

Role: As a Catholic priest in the early sixteenth century, Martin Luther was best known for challenging the authority of the Catholic Church. He became a significant force in the Reformation and inspired the development of new Protestant sects of Christianity.

After a year, Luther moved to Eisenach to live with relatives and attended the parish school at St. George. Although he received good grades at school and was well liked by his classmates, he is thought to have suffered from depression, a condition that plagued him for most of his life.

Life in the Religious Order

The monks at the monastery woke up every morning at 2:00. They worked or worshipped until their first meal (lunch), which was one of only two meals per day. Monks could not talk to one another, so they had to use a sort of sign language to communicate. They walked with their hands hidden in their sleeves and their eyes on the ground, and they were not allowed to have any contact with women.

Preparation for the Reformation. Luther's father saved enough money to send him to the renowned university at Erfurt, the second largest city in Germany. Luther began his studies in law and liberal arts in 1501, at the age of eighteen; he earned a bachelor's degree in one year, then a master's degree two years later.

Hans Luder was thrilled at his son's success in school and hoped that the aspiring student's pursuit of a career in law would raise the status of the whole family. Luther had just begun his law studies when the plague struck Germany. Two of his brothers were killed by the disease, and the university was temporarily closed. He returned home until the plague subsided, then started back to the university.

A vision. Luther was traveling back to Erfurt by foot when he was caught in a thunderstorm. He is said to have seen a terrifying vision that convinced him to give up law and join a monastery instead. Shocked by a thunderbolt in the midst of the storm, he proclaimed, "St. Anne help me! I will become a monk!" (Bainton, p. 15). Luther apparently offered his service to God in exchange for surviving the storm.

Dedication to religious life. Upon his return to Erfurt, Luther immediately sold all of his new law books. That same night, he invited over several of his friends for dinner, then went directly to the Augustinian monastery in town.

Initially Luther's parents were upset by his change in career plans. They later softened their views on the subject and gave him their blessing. In 1507 Luther took the vows of poverty, chastity, and obedience and became a priest.

Problems with the church. Corruption rocked the Catholic Church in the fifteenth and sixteenth centuries. Religion became a profitable business, and unscrupulous church officials began to charge people for "indulgences," or forgiveness from their sins. Some priests and bishops deliberately fostered the image of a cruel God; frightened into repentance, members of their congregations were then more willing to pay higher and higher prices for indulgences. Luther was disturbed by the portrait of a wrathful God and felt torn by the growing conflicts in the Catholic Church.

Priest and professor. In the winter of 1511-12 Luther became embroiled in a controversy surrounding the merger of his religious order with another, more liberal order. This was the first time Luther defied the authority of the church, though it would not be the last. As a result of his opposition to the merger, he was sent to teach philosophy at the university at Wittenberg, where he met John (Johann von) Staupitz, a high church official. Staupitz convinced Luther that there was no reason to fear God and encouraged him to interpret the Bible for himself.

Writings of Martin Luther

The 95 theses was just the first of Luther's writings crusading for church reform. As his teachings drew more attention, he wrote articles challenging the leaders of nations and states to push for reform in the church. One article called for a march on Rome to purge the church of its pope, whom Luther labeled the anti-Christ. The church soon published a notice, a papal bull, warning him to stop his teaching on the threat of excommunication. When Luther received this notice, he burned it. He was excommunicated in 1521.

A new view of God. With the guidance and encouragement of Staupitz, Luther came to see God as a loving savior. He concluded that absolute faith was the key to salvation. (This doctrine of faith eventually became the central belief of Protestantism.) For the rest of his life, Luther lectured on theology, gave sermons at the town church, and wrote about the Bible and the state of the Catholic Church.

Public criticism of the church. Luther first voiced his dissatisfaction with the Catholic Church in a 1517 sermon he gave against the sale of indulgences. He later put his criticisms of the church in writing and nailed them to the door of the cathedral in Wittenberg. These criticisms, called the 95 theses, challenged the

▲ Luther nailing his 95 theses to the door of the cathedral in Wittenberg; these criticisms challenged the absolute authority of the pope and sparked the Reformation movement in Germany.

absolute authority of the pope and sparked the Reformation movement in Germany.

Luther tried to work within the structure of the Catholic Church to make the changes he felt were necessary, but church officials accused him of heresy. His dissent inspired many Catholics to rebel against the church and led to the formation of a new branch of Christianity known as "Protestantism"—so named because it was born out of a "protest" against Roman Catholicism.

Working within the church. Luther spent the rest of his life struggling to reform the Catholic Church. He discouraged the separation of Protestants from Catholics and argued for a rational examination of the deep-seated problems that were destroying the church. He was quoted as saying: "We have to act as good children whose parents have lost their minds" (Gritsch, p. 33).

Controversy over the Reformation led to violence. At one point, Luther was tried before Emperor Charles V and banned from society because of his religious teachings. Orders were sent out for his capture, and he was haunted by the knowledge that he might be killed at any time.

For almost a year, he lived in seclusion at a castle in a German forest; he grew a beard and called himself "Knight George." When the furor died down, he returned to society and continued his criticisms of the church. He also translated the Old and New Testaments into German so that people throughout the country could read the Bible for themselves. Luther's refreshing interpretations of the scriptures inspired monks, nuns, and lay people to abandon traditional church values and seek a more direct relationship with God. By speaking out against the corrupt officials of the Catholic Church, Luther had caused a religious revolution.

Conflicting ideas on marriage. Luther's views on marriage ran contrary to the teachings of the Catholic Church. He felt that nuns and priests could marry without compromising their commitment to God and their congregations. In 1525 he and Katharina von Bora, a former nun, were wed. They made a life for themselves on land that had previously belonged to the monastery in Wittenberg, had six children together, and took in four orphans. Luther continued to give lectures and sermons and write essays until he died—most likely from heart failure—at the age of sixty-two.

Later Works

After his return to work at the university, Luther proposed changes to the sacraments held by the Catholic Church. There had been seven, but he thought only two should be kept. He also wrote a recommendation for a new church government, giving greater authority to civil rulers. One of his best-known writings, however, was a song—"A Mighty Fortress Is Our God"—which is sung in almost all Protestant churches to this day.

Aftermath

Luther's views and actions gave rise to the Reformation and

▲ Martin Luther burns the papal bull threatening him with excommunication; Luther's actions triggered a peasant revolt in Europe—and with it the realization of reformed church ideas.

the various branches of Protestantism. He left behind volumes of essays that helped shape the Reformation and continue to inspire people of the Christian faith at the dawn of the twenty-first century. Luther's legacy in Protestantism influenced the history of European, South American, and U.S. religions. His teachings split Germany, as the rulers of some states finally united to begin the first of the organized Protestant churches in a sect called Lutheranism.

Luther's ideas were indeed revolutionary. He showed how politics and business could distort Christianity. However, it was not until centuries later that the separation of church and state would become a worldwide standard.

Atkinson, James. *Martin Luther: Prophet to the Church Catholic.* New York: Books Demand, 1983.

Bainton, Ronald H. *Here I Stand: A Life of Martin Luther.* Nashville, Tennessee: Festival Books, 1978.

Gritsch, Eric W. *Luther—God's Court Jester: Luther in Retrospect.* Philadelphia: Fortress Press, 1983.

Loewenich, Walter von. *Martin Luther: The Man and His Works.* Translated by Lawrence W. Denef. Augsburg: Augsburg Fortress, 1989.

Luther, Martin. *Selections from His Writings.* Edited by John Dillenberger. Garden City, New York: Doubleday, 1958.

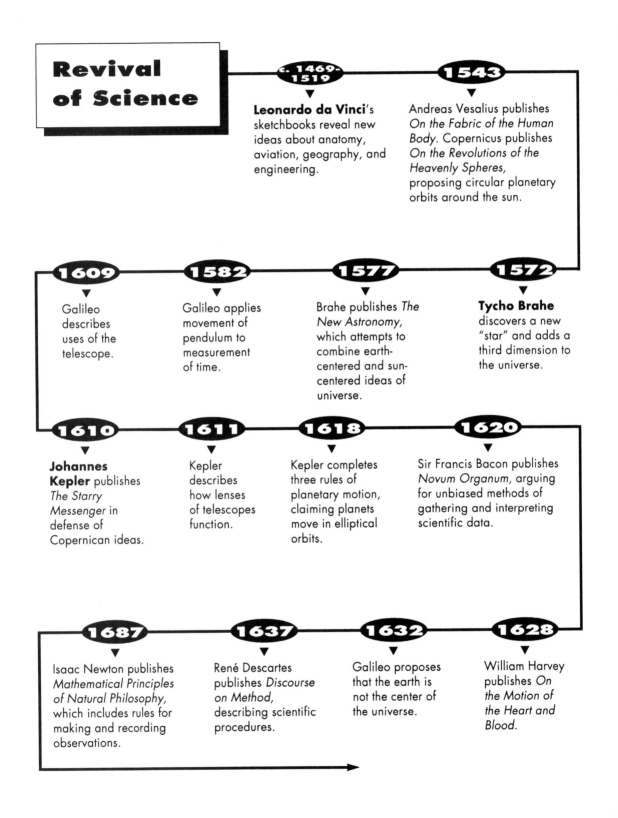

Revival of Science

c. 1469-1519
Leonardo da Vinci's sketchbooks reveal new ideas about anatomy, aviation, geography, and engineering.

1543
Andreas Vesalius publishes *On the Fabric of the Human Body*. Copernicus publishes *On the Revolutions of the Heavenly Spheres*, proposing circular planetary orbits around the sun.

1609
Galileo describes uses of the telescope.

1582
Galileo applies movement of pendulum to measurement of time.

1577
Brahe publishes *The New Astronomy*, which attempts to combine earth-centered and sun-centered ideas of universe.

1572
Tycho Brahe discovers a new "star" and adds a third dimension to the universe.

1610
Johannes Kepler publishes *The Starry Messenger* in defense of Copernican ideas.

1611
Kepler describes how lenses of telescopes function.

1618
Kepler completes three rules of planetary motion, claiming planets move in elliptical orbits.

1620
Sir Francis Bacon publishes *Novum Organum*, arguing for unbiased methods of gathering and interpreting scientific data.

1687
Isaac Newton publishes *Mathematical Principles of Natural Philosophy*, which includes rules for making and recording observations.

1637
René Descartes publishes *Discourse on Method*, describing scientific procedures.

1632
Galileo proposes that the earth is not the center of the universe.

1628
William Harvey publishes *On the Motion of the Heart and Blood*.

REVIVAL OF SCIENCE

The Renaissance encouraged great individual achievements in all areas of human endeavor, but no area was affected more deeply or more permanently than philosophy—the study of the nature of the universe and humanity's place in it. Science, a new field of philosophy, was explored by scholars who based their ideas on objective investigation and the gathering and recording of measurable data. As the new scientific method evolved, perhaps few notions were so drastically altered as those held by philosophers interested in celestial events.

The importance of astronomy. Throughout the fifteenth and sixteenth centuries, many people believed that certain aspects of their lives were controlled by the heavenly bodies. Astronomy (the name for the science of the celestial bodies) first captured the interest of the Babylonians and the Greeks hundreds of years before the birth of Christ. The early Greeks had given a clear view of the arrangement of these bodies—locked in a spherical pattern circling the earth—and this pattern was used to develop ideas about the significance of the locations of planets at any given time. It was important to know these locations in order to predict the best time to pray, make contracts, give birth, or even die. Astronomy was among the subjects at the forefront

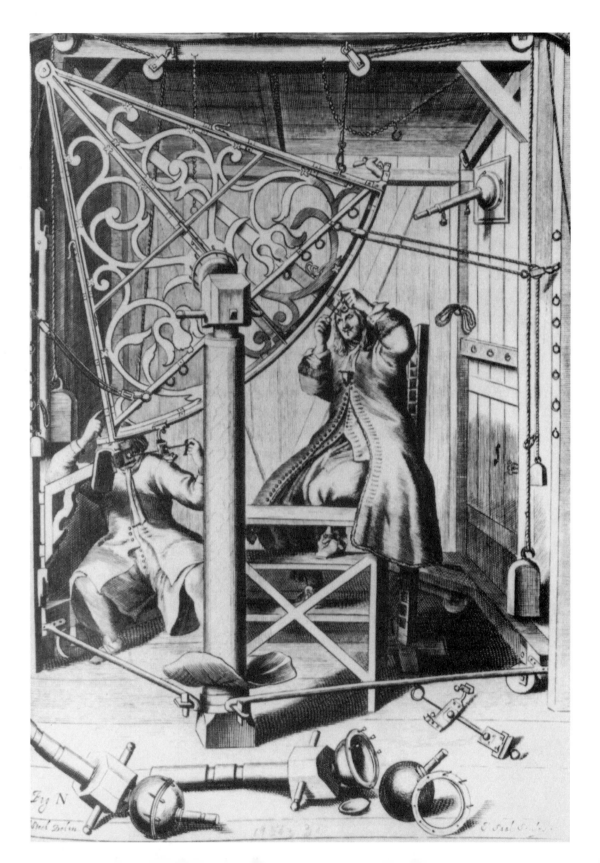

Fig. N

of a growing intellectual revolution. But the Renaissance, or "rebirth" of the classics, first showed itself in the arts.

Merging information. One of the great artists of the Renaissance, **Leonardo da Vinci,** adhered to methods that came to be associated with modern science, namely the meticulous observation and recording of data. Leonardo learned about muscle structure by dissecting a human body and then applied this knowledge to the creation of lifelike sculptures. By carefully observing the motions of a flying bird and applying the laws of mathematics and engineering, he created a human flying machine. These ideas and more were recorded in the Leonardo notebooks. Thus Leonardo da Vinci became a model for future builders of the new science.

Sixteenth-century Danish astronomer **Tycho Brahe** directed the construction of one of the world's greatest observatories. With pre-telescopic tools, he measured the positions of planets and even discovered a new star. But Brahe's devotion to religion led him to believe that the earth was at the center of the universe because it housed human beings, God's greatest creation. He spent most of his life trying to reconcile the differences between what his religion taught and what his mathematics revealed. Brahe championed the notion that data should be gathered over a period of time and from different points of view. He made some of the most accurate measurements possible at that time of planets and their motions.

Meanwhile, other scientists were busy defining new methods of scientific investigation. In England, Sir Francis Bacon called for objective data gathering. True scientists, he held, should not gather information to prove a position they already held but to challenge their own thoughts. Isaac Newton published a refinement of this theory in a book laying out rules for making observations. These rules came to be known as the scientific method.

◄

An astronomer and his assistant, from Johannes Hevel's *Machina coelestis,* **1679; astronomy was among the subjects at the forefront of the growing intellectual revolution.**

▲ Leonardo da Vinci's drawing of a wing-testing rig for an ornithopter wing, 1486-90; by carefully observing the motions of a flying bird, Leonardo created a human flying machine.

Around the same time, scientists were developing better and better tools for observation. Galileo adapted the earlier-known lens to create a telescope that brought the heavenly bodies closer into view. In Holland, other students were working on the creation of a microscopic lens.

Meanwhile, Brahe's assistant, **Johannes Kepler,** inherited his mentor's carefully drawn data, added more of his own, and applied his great mathematical skills to measurements of the planets. His mathematical models at first gave no more suitable explanation of planetary motion than Brahe had given. But eventually Kepler was able to provide the modern picture of planets moving around the sun in elliptical orbits. In 1637, nearly two hundred years after Leonardo, another scientist, René Descartes, published *Discourse on Method,* a pivotal volume that is widely regarded as the beginning point of modern science.

Leonardo da Vinci

1452-1519

Personal Background

Early life. Leonardo da Vinci was born in Anchiano, Italy, on April 15, 1452, to Piero da Vinci, a prominent public official in Florence, and a peasant woman named Caterina. Shortly after his birth, both parents married, but not to each other. Caterina wed a man named Antonio, and Piero married Albiera di Giovanni Amadori. As an infant, Leonardo was cared for by Piero's mother, Lucia, and his uncle, Francesco. Later, his father took him into his own house, where he joined half-brothers and half-sisters in receiving the best education Piero could provide. Leonardo was particularly fascinated with the study of mechanics and music. Socially, he is said to have been one of the most popular young men of Florence.

Apprenticeship. In 1466 Leonardo was apprenticed to Andrea del Verrocchio, a man who would have a profound influence on the young boy's life. Verrocchio was a master painter and sculptor, and his studio was much like a technical college. Students there not only learned painting and sculpting techniques but also bronze casting, stone masonry, drafting, architecture, building, and engineering.

The education Leonardo received from Verrocchio was very practical. He learned art as a science that involved mathematics, chemistry, and even architecture. Instead of studying art tech-

▲ **Leonardo da Vinci**

Event: Merging art and science.

Role: Leonardo da Vinci merged his interests in science and the arts to produce one of the most extensive and influential bodies of work ever compiled in one lifetime. Though best known as a master painter, Leonardo had a great impact on aviation, anatomy, architecture, mechanics, mathematics, physics, optics, engineering, and astronomy.

niques in books, Leonardo practiced painting, sculpting, and building his own works and assisted Verrocchio as well.

One of Leonardo's first projects was to help his teacher build a golden sphere and cross to sit atop the domed cathedral of Santa Maria del Fiori, an outstanding structure for the fifteenth century. It was a huge undertaking that required complicated mathematical calculations and casting techniques. The project taught Leonardo that scientific knowledge and art could work hand in hand.

The influence of Florence. The city of Florence also had a marked impact on Leonardo's life. There he was exposed to the Italian Renaissance (a period of accelerated interest in literature, art, and learning characterized by a "rebirth" of the classics). At the time, Florence was a large, industrial urban area known for its technological achievements. It also housed many scholars, artists, and scientists, some of whom had been driven there by the fall of Constantinople to the Turks. This diversely talented population brought a wealth of new ideas to the city. Great thinkers, including Verrocchio himself, gathered in Florence to seek answers to the pressing questions of the day.

The thought and activity going on all around him sparked a great curiosity in Leonardo. He stretched his thinking beyond art to other areas. For example, Florence was a center of the silk trade; Leonardo invented a machine for spinning silk into weaving thread. He also created plans to change the paths of larger rivers and to build canals that would improve trade between Florence and other cities. In addition, he learned about anatomy and dissection from Antonio Pollaiuolo, an artist who occupied the studio next to Verrocchio.

As a nature-lover, Leonardo was known to frequent the open markets of Florence, purchasing caged birds and setting them

A Few of Leonardo's Achievements as a Scientist

Anatomy: Dissected a human body and sketched muscles in order to achieve accuracy in his sculptures.

Aviation: Observed the flights of birds and drew plans for a flying machine.

Biology: Made observations of animals, particularly their movements; wrote a paper on the shape of a horse.

Engineering: Designed canals around the city of Milan; invented an early version of a machine gun; designed warheads.

Geology: Studied rock formations and drew pictures to show the actions of waterfalls.

free. Though most often a resident of Italy's cities, he preserved a deep appreciation of the natural world and a respect for living things that can be seen in his paintings.

Accredited artist. By age twenty, Leonardo had established himself firmly in the art world and was accepted into the guild of Florentine artists. However, he continued to work under Verrocchio for another ten years. The teacher and his student had a remarkable relationship. Verrocchio allowed him great freedom to experiment in his varied interests, and Leonardo apparently was content to let Verrocchio get the bulk of the credit for his work.

Though he was already a master painter in his own right and could have begun his own studio, Leonardo was not concerned with wealth or fame. (In fact, he rarely even signed his paintings; consequently, most of the work he did before the age of thirty has been lost or never identified.) He remained with Verrocchio until 1483, when he moved to Milan.

> ## Leonardo's "Secret Code"
>
> Leonardo wrote from right to left and often in code; his notebooks had to be read with a mirror and often could not be deciphered at all. It is believed that this practice started because he was left-handed and as a child wrote naturally from right to left. Most likely he continued to write that way as an adult because he realized the value of keeping his ideas secret.

Participation: Merging Art and Science

Milan. At this point, Leonardo considered himself more of an engineer than a painter. Selling himself as a highly creative military engineer, he went to work for Ludovico Sforza (known as "il Moro," the Moor), ruler of the city. He confidently told Sforza, who was then at war with Venice:

> I have plans for bridges.... I can make armored vehicles, safe and unassailable ... [and I have] plans for destroying fortifications inaccessible to cannon.... In short, as the variety of circumstances necessitate, I can supply an infinite number of different engines of attack and defense. (Zubov, p. 11)

Leonardo added that he could also be of value in times of peace as an artist whose work "will stand in comparison with that of anyone else" (Zubov, p. 11).

▲ *The Last Supper,* Leonardo's mural in the monastery of Santa Maria della Grazie in Milan.

Sforza gladly hired Leonardo and put him to work re-fortifying the castle of Milan and planning bridges and canals. Leonardo also served as the court architect, or designer, organizing festivals and jousting competitions, building a revolving stage, and remodeling the grounds. All these activities enhanced his knowledge of mathematics, mechanics, and physics, and he soon began developing and testing his own inventions and theories.

A burst of creativity. His first stay in Milan—from 1483 to 1499—proved to be one of the most creative of his life. He filled notebooks with questions on all branches of science and studied ancient scholarly texts in an effort to build on the lessons of past geniuses.

Unending curiosity. Leonardo's unending curiosity and creativity led him to produce an amazing amount of work on all fronts. He developed theorems in geometry—most notably the discovery of how to determine the center of gravity of a pyramid. He described the shapes of sections of cones without ever having attended a single university class in mathematics. He made sketches of human anatomy and wrote a paper specifically on the nervous system, called "the tree of veins," that remains one of the best investigations of the topic ever completed. Leonardo also made breakthroughs in astronomy, observing, for instance, that moonlight is reflected light and that the earth spins on its own axis. While studying the flight of birds, he conceived a plan for a "flying apparatus," a sort of blueprint for the modern-day helicopter. At the same time, Leonardo completed one of his greatest artistic masterpieces, *The Last Supper*, for the dining room of Santa Maria della Grazie.

Unfinished works. Though Leonardo clearly possessed enormous talent and energy in a wide range of subjects and projects, he seldom finished what he started. For example, when he developed his mathematical theories, he put them to practical use but never bothered to publish them. Leonardo had little interest in gaining fame or fortune for his discoveries, and seems to have moved on to other ideas as soon as he felt he had grasped a given subject. Because he never proved his theories by gathering and publishing his data, he was given little credit for his scientific discoveries during his lifetime. In fact, a great deal of his work was not uncovered until well into the eighteenth and nineteenth centuries, when his notebooks were finally published. The same holds true for Leonardo's art. Many of his paintings and sculptures were never completed; as a result, only a few of his masterpieces exist today.

The Mystery of the Mona Lisa

The *Mona Lisa*, or *La Giaconda*, is one of the great mysteries of the art world. Previously believed to have been painted in 1503, it is now thought to have been completed sometime between 1514 and 1516. Just who posed for the painting is as controversial as the date. Among the possible models are Francesco del Giocondo (a nobleman's wife who may have inspired the name of the painting) or one of two duchesses—the Duchess Constanza d'Avalos or Pacifica—both mistresses of Giuliano de Medici, a friend of Leonardo's in Rome. One thing is certain: the *Mona Lisa* is Leonardo's most famous work. The painting today hangs in the Louvre in Paris, France.

Return to Florence. In 1499 the French invaded Milan and killed Leonardo's patron, Sforza. Leonardo moved back to Florence and for the next six years focused most of his energy on exploring geometry, anatomy, and engineering. In 1502 and 1503 he worked

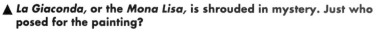 **▲ *La Giaconda,* or the *Mona Lisa,* is shrouded in mystery. Just who posed for the painting?**

for Cesare Borgia as a military engineer and mapped the Italian coast. The maps he produced display his great talent for merging science and art. More than mere trip routes, they include depictions of plants, countryside, minerals, and rock formations—all painted with great detail and skill.

Second visit to Milan. At the request of Charles d'Amboise, French ruler of Milan, Leonardo returned to that city as a painter in 1507. Over the next five years, he painted well-known works: *Leda, St. Anne,* and *John the Baptist.* He also completed an elaborate garden for his patron that included fountains, canals, and showers. Leonardo's notes on the project show that he was even trying to find a way to "pipe in" music and capture the fragrant scent of citrus trees within the garden walls.

In 1512 Leonardo left Milan. He settled briefly in Rome and then in Cloux, France, to work for King Francis I. Around this time, he painted the famous *Mona Lisa.*

Aftermath

Death. During the last years of his life, Leonardo worked for Francis I, who felt that "no other man had been born into the world who knew as much as Leonardo" (Zubov, p. 39). Because he developed a paralysis in his arm, the artist painted very little after 1516. Instead, he designed a new court for his patron and planned a series of canals that would connect the Loire and Seine rivers. On April 23, 1518, he made a will leaving his work to Francesco de Melzi, who had been his student for many years. On May 2, 1519, the great scholar died at the age of sixty-seven.

An artistic and scientific genius, Leonardo had a deep effect on the world and helped usher in both the Renaissance and the scientific revolution. As a scientific thinker he was unsurpassed for centuries, and as a painter he remains one of the great masters—"one of the first to realize the soft texture of the skin" and picture it on canvas (Philipsson, p. 56).

For More Information

Philipsson, Morris. *Leonardo da Vinci: Aspects of the Renaissance Genius.* New York: George Braziller, 1966.

Richter, John Paul, editor. *The Literary Works of Leonardo da Vinci.* Vols. 1 and 2. Berkeley: University of California Press, 1977.

Zubov, V. P. *Leonardo da Vinci.* Cambridge: Harvard University Press, 1968.

Tycho Brahe

1546-1601

Personal Background

Tyge "Tycho" Brahe was born December 14, 1546, in Knudstrup, Scania, Denmark. (The city of his birth is now part of Sweden.) He was the second child and the eldest son of Otto and Beate Bille Brahe's ten children.

Raised by uncle. The Brahes were an ancient noble family of Sweden and Denmark. Tycho spent the first year of his life with his father and mother before being kidnapped by his paternal uncle, Jorgen Brahe. The young boy then lived with his prosperous uncle on a country estate at Tostrup.

Education. Beginning at age seven, Brahe was privately tutored in Latin, basic math, reading, and writing. He took a keen interest in Latin and poetry and began composing his own verses at an early age. When he turned thirteen, Brahe was sent to the University of Copenhagen to study rhetoric and philosophy—all in preparation for becoming a statesman in the Brahe family tradition. But it soon became apparent that Brahe would not follow tradition and would instead forge his own path in the world.

Eclipse of 1560. While Brahe was at the University of Copenhagen, a natural event took place that changed his life. On August 21, 1560, there was an eclipse of the sun. Brahe was fascinated by it and began consulting with professors of science at the university.

▲ Tycho Brahe

Event: Merging technology and science.

Role: Known as the "reformer of observational astronomy," Tycho Brahe recorded celestial observations that greatly advanced the knowledge of the universe and enabled fellow astronomer Johannes Kepler to discover the laws of planetary motion. Brahe was the first to realize that continuous and systematic observations of celestial bodies were crucial to understanding the true motions of stars and planets.

SEXTANS ASTRONOMICUS TRIGONICUS
PRO DISTANTIIS RIMANDIS.

▲ With a sextant (pictured here) and other measuring instruments, Brahe recorded the movement and color changes of stars and calculated their distances.

Leap at Leipzig. In 1562 Brahe went to the University of Leipzig in Germany—fertile ground for the study of astronomy. He was accompanied by a tutor, Anders Sorensen Vedel. In addition to his teaching duties, Vedel was paid to encourage Brahe's pursuit of a career as a diplomat, not an astronomer.

To appease his tutor and his family, Brahe studied law by day but indulged in the study of astronomy by night. He discovered major flaws in all of the tables then available on the topic of celestial movement and concluded that only through continuous and systematic observation of heavenly bodies could celestial motion be accurately predicted. Today this seems like a simple and logical statement, but at the time it was a bold revelation. Because Vedel controlled Brahe's finances, the young scientist had to construct his own crude instruments to assist him in his observations. As he increased his familiarity with astronomical tools, Brahe became convinced that no device—no matter how well made—could guarantee error-free measurement. Consequently, the young astronomer designed mathematic tables to adjust his measurements for these built-in errors. By the mid-1560s Brahe was recording his observations of the stars and planets—observations that would revolutionize the science and practice of astronomy.

Duel of 1566. Some biographers suggest that Brahe was a very arrogant and egotistical young scientist. This attitude may have contributed to a pivotal event in his life—one that had little to do with astronomy. On December 10, 1566, Brahe and mathematician Marderup Parsberg got into an argument at a party, perhaps over a mathematical point. On December 27, the two quarreled again and decided to settle their argument with a duel. Two days later, the duel took place; Brahe suffered the greatest injury, losing part of his nose to a swipe of Marderup's

Astronomy in the 15th Century

In Tycho Brahe's day, it was commonly believed that the planets controlled health, destiny, and other earthly matters such as weather and natural disasters. Brahe himself was very interested in "judicial astrology" and made horoscopes for his friends and nobility based on celestial movements. Some of Brahe's predictions were apparently right on target: he is said to have predicted mathematician Caspar Peucer's imprisonment and eventual freedom, and he was noted for his accuracy in predicting rain. However, when one of his predictions—the death of a Turkish sultan—was made after the ruler had already died, Brahe became the butt of many jokes.

▲ Postage stamp showing Brahe's observatory, Uraniborg; the star he discovered in 1572; and his quadrant, a tool used for measuring the altitude of stars.

sword. From then on, he wore a piece made of gold and silver over his nose to conceal the injury. It is said that he constructed this "false nose" himself and carried with him a small container of wax to re-affix it when it came unhinged. Aside from his scientific contributions, Brahe was most well known for his metal nose.

Participation:
Merging Technology and Science

Star of 1572. Brahe returned to Denmark to see his ailing father in late 1570. Upon his father's death, he inherited some family property and moved into Heridsvad Abbey, where he set up a makeshift observatory. Now free from family intervention in his career choice, he could openly indulge in astronomy. His first major observation came in 1572, when he discovered a new star in the constellation of Cassiopeia. With a sextant and several other measuring instruments he had constructed while in college, Brahe recorded the movement and color change of the star and roughly calculated its distance. For eighteen months he systemat-

▲ Brahe's observatory, Uraniborg, attracted scholars and scientists from throughout Europe who visited and apprenticed under the esteemed astronomer.

ically recorded his observations of the star until it disappeared from plain view in March 1574.

Scholars urged Brahe to publish his findings, but noblemen of the sixteenth century rarely spent their time writing books. However, when other astronomers began publishing incorrect data on the star of 1572, Brahe felt compelled to put forth his own account. His 1573 book *De Nova Stella* ("On the New Star") thrust him into the forefront of contemporary astronomy. Brahe's observations were far superior to any others known, and his estimation

that the star was located at a distance much farther than the moon revolutionized thinking on the location of planets and stars.

Marriage and Hveen. The year that his work was published, Brahe fell in love with a commoner named Christine. Though the two did not officially marry, their union was bound by common law and lasted twenty-six years. Together they had eight children, six of whom survived childhood.

For three years, at the request of Danish King Frederick II, Brahe lectured at the University of Copenhagen on planetary motion; he was granted a house and observatory on the isle of Hveen (now Ven), fourteen miles north of Copenhagen in the North Sea. Frederick made Brahe ruler of the whole small island and its inhabitants. He thus became a landlord over a village and about forty farms and could collect taxes from them. Brahe used the money to construct and equip an observatory, which he called "Uraniborg" after the muse of astronomy Urania. Completed in 1580, the observatory attracted scholars and scientists from throughout Europe who visited and apprenticed under the esteemed astronomer.

Most productive years. For the next twenty years, Brahe and his students charted the course of the planets and catalogued more than a thousand stars—all without the aid of a telescope. Brahe commissioned the construction of a printing press (a newly invented piece of machinery) and published all of his findings himself. His first major book was on the comet of 1577 and the system of the world. By proving the existence of the new star of 1572 and the comet of 1577, Brahe established that new bodies could appear in so-called "aethereal" regions. This demolished Aristotle's argument that no new bodies could exist in these regions and established Brahe as the leading authority on such questions.

Tychonic System. Brahe continued his observations and eventually published his own "system" or theory of planetary

◄
An illustration from Brahe's *Epistolarum*, 1596; Brahe commissioned the construction of a printing press and published all of his findings himself.

movement in a book called *Astronomic Instauratae Progymnasmata* or "The New Astronomy." His "Tychonic System," as it came to be called, combined the Copernican theory of a "heliocentric" or sun-centered universe with the theory of a "geocentric" or earth-centered universe. Brahe believed that all the planets but Earth revolved around the sun, and the sun revolved around the Earth. Not surprisingly, Brahe's complex system was never widely accepted. However, he changed the practice of astronomy with his claim that heavenly bodies must be systematically observed over time in order to extend knowledge. From that point on, scientists only proposed theories that could be backed up by observations. Because of Brahe, astronomy became a practical, not a theoretical science—truly a "new astronomy."

Lord of Uraniborg

In addition to the observatory Uraniborg, Brahe oversaw the construction of other buildings on Hveen, including a large house, an alchemy laboratory, a prison, a building for his own printing press, and servants' quarters. Brahe's kingdom was surrounded by a massive earthen wall. Inside the wall, Brahe lived lavishly. Some accounts tell of his large dining table under which a clown (perhaps a dwarf) crouched during meals and ate the droppings from the table.

Aftermath

Exile to Bohemia. In 1588 King Frederick II died, and thereafter Brahe fell out of favor with the Danish royalty. Described as a "fiery" man, he had never dealt with authority very well, and after a final quarrel over funding, he left Hveen and Denmark for Bohemia. Emperor Rudolf II, an avid supporter of science and art, invited Brahe to Prague and extended an invitation for the famed astronomer to construct an observatory at one of his castles. Virtually exiled from his homeland, Brahe accepted the emperor's offer and moved his family to Benatky Castle, twenty-two miles east of Prague.

Kepler and fate. Once he had settled in Bohemia, Brahe made contact with fellow astronomer Johannes Kepler. The course of scientific history forever changed because of their meeting.

Kepler had just written a very influential book on the distances of the planets from the sun (based on the Copernican system) and sent a copy to Brahe. Though the two differed over their concepts of the organization of the universe, they admired each other's ideas. Further, Kepler realized that Brahe was aging and that no one had yet tapped the vast knowledge and information he possessed from his decades of observation. Kepler approached Brahe about working together, and Brahe eagerly accepted him as an assistant in 1600.

For the next year, Kepler pored over Brahe's volumes of observations and worked with him on his *Progymnasmata* and *Rudolphine Tables* (tables of planetary movements and distances). By this time, Brahe was already very weak. Within a few months, he was near death. He willed his life's work to Kepler and implored him to finish the *Tables* on his own. On October 24, 1601, Brahe died at the age of fifty-four, but because of his union with Kepler, his work lived on.

Legacy. Tycho Brahe was laid to rest with enormous pomp and circumstance befitting "a king among astronomers" (Dreyer, p. 363). He revolutionized the practice of astronomy and believed that the study of the heavens lifted man above earthly and trivial things. Brahe's painstaking observations enabled Kepler to come up with the laws of planetary motion and laid the foundation of modern astronomy, which is based on regular and systematic celestial observation.

Brahe the Poet

In addition to being a brilliant scientist, Brahe enjoyed composing poetry. Mostly written in Latin, Brahe's verses usually praised his observatory or paid homage to great astronomers of the past, such as Copernicus and Ptolemy. Often he had his poems inscribed over the entrances to his observatories; such was the case at Hveen and Benatky.

For More Information

Dreyer, J. L. E. *Tycho Brahe: A Picture of Scientific Life and Work in the Sixteenth Century.* Edinburgh: Adam & Charles Black, 1890.

Lodge, Oliver. *Pioneers of Science.* London: St. Martin's, 1913.

Ronan, Colin. *The Astronomers.* New York: Hill & Wang, 1964.

Williams, Henry Smith. *The Great Astronomers.* New York: Newton, 1932.

Johannes Kepler

1571-1630

Personal Background

Johannes "John" Kepler was born to a poor family in Weil, near Würtemburg, Germany on December 17, 1571. His father served as a soldier in the duke's army and later owned a tavern where Johannes was employed from ages nine to twelve. His mother, Catherine, who was noted for her fiery temperament, also worked at the tavern and cared for her home and family.

Smallpox. When Kepler was only four years old, he suffered a severe attack of smallpox. The illness did permanent damage to his eyesight and left him very weak. For the rest of his life he was unable to go out at night because of his frail constitution. With outdoor activities severely limited, Kepler turned to reading and writing. He was fascinated by numbers and geometry and continually asked questions—especially about the way the universe worked.

Education. At the age of seventeen Kepler enrolled at the University of Tübingen, where he studied astronomy and theology and graduated second in his class. In college he was exposed to the ideas of Copernicus, the first astronomer to assert that the sun was the center of our solar system. The Catholic Church at that time held that the earth was the center of the universe, so Copernicus's position was strongly opposed. But Kepler believed in Copernicus's model and defended it in debates at his university.

▲ Johannes Kepler

Event: Revival of science and math in Europe.

Role: Using Tycho Brahe's lifetime of celestial observations, Johannes Kepler developed three laws of planetary motion that revolutionized astronomy and led to Sir Isaac Newton's discovery of the laws of gravity.

▲ Kepler's drawings show his fascination with numbers and geometry. Geometric shapes may have helped him to visualize various relationships of time and space.

He earned a master's degree in 1591 and for the next two years worked within the Lutheran Church. Like his mother, however, Kepler had a fiery disposition, and he clashed with Lutheran authorities over the strictness of the church. In 1594, when the opportunity arose for him to teach astronomy at the University of Gratz, he left the church and became a professor.

Life of a sixteenth-century astronomer. During the sixteenth century, astronomy was closely tied to astrology. It was believed that the stars and planets dictated human destiny and controlled everything from weather patterns to political events. Therefore, the job of the astronomer was not only to make accurate calendars but to forecast weather, prepare horoscopes, and make political predictions. Kepler's first years at Gratz were spent pursuing these activities, but he also spent long nights poring over books, making calculations, and guessing as to the nature of the universe.

First book and theory. Kepler sought to find a connection between the number of planets (then it was believed there were only six: Mercury, Venus, Earth, Mars, Jupiter, and Saturn), their times of revolution, and their distance from the sun. In his 1596 publication *Mysterium Cosmographicum,* he put forth his "regular-solid" hypothesis describing such a connection. Though the hypothesis was flawed, at the time it was widely acclaimed and helped establish Kepler as a first-rate astronomer and intellectual. After years of hard work and calculation, he was thrilled at his first discovery and wrote:

> The intense pleasure I have received from this discovery can never be told in words. I regretted no more the time wasted; I tired of no labour; I shunned no toil of reckoning, of days and nights spent in calculation, until I could see whether my hypothesis would agree with the orbits of Copernicus, or whether my joy was to vanish in air. (Lodge, p. 62)

A Witch in the Family?

Later in her life, Kepler's mother Catherine was involved in a lawsuit. The person she was suing had accused her of witchcraft. She was convicted and sentenced to a year of prison and torture. Kepler returned to Würtemburg to come to her defense. Though he was unable to free her from jail, he did succeed in preventing her from being tortured. However, when she was freed she again pursued the lawsuit.

The book captured the attention of two famed astronomers, Tycho Brahe and Galileo Galilei, who would later become very involved in Kepler's life and enable his greatest achievements.

Participation:
Revival of Science and Math in Europe

Brahe and brilliance. Though Kepler had always been a brilliant thinker, he lacked the data to calculate, develop, and prove his theories. After his first book came out, he began corresponding with Danish astronomer Tycho Brahe, who had spent more than twenty years compiling celestial observations.

Kepler sent Brahe a copy of his book and the two began corresponding by letter. Though Brahe had an idea about the organization of the solar system that was very different from that of Copernicus and Kepler, he greatly respected Kepler's work. For several years, the two had friendly and frank exchanges in which Brahe continually tried to convert Kepler to his "Tychonic System" (a theory that all the planets but Earth revolved around the sun, and the sun revolved around the Earth) and Kepler politely but forcefully refused.

When Kepler was forced to leave his teaching position at Gratz in 1599, he called on Brahe, who was then Imperial Mathematician of the Holy Roman Empire. Brahe was by this time old and weak, and Kepler realized that no one had yet tapped his vast store of knowledge. He offered to examine Brahe's compilation of observations and use them to perfect theories of planetary motion. Brahe eagerly accepted Kepler's proposal, saying: "Come not as a stranger, but as a very welcome friend; come and share in my observations with such instruments as I have with me, and as a dearly beloved associate" (Lodge, p. 63).

> ### The Rudolphine Tables
>
> Astronomers with differing points of view about how the solar system was organized developed tables of movements and distances of celestial bodies according to their individual views. Brahe and Kepler developed the *Rudolphine Tables*—named after the emperor who sponsored them—on the theory that the planets revolved around the sun in elliptical orbits.

Kepler's first two laws of planetary motion. The timing could not have been better for the meeting of two such brilliant minds. Brahe was near death, and Kepler was able to access his lifetime of work before he passed away. Brahe put Kepler to work calculating the movements of Mars. Kepler also worked with Brahe on the *Rudolphine Tables* (which described planetary movements) and pledged, as the older astronomer's health worsened, that he would complete them. After Brahe's passing in 1601, Kepler was named Imperial Mathematician and continued to work at Brahe's observatory at Benatky Castle.

For six years Kepler struggled to explain the way the planets move. He described his quest in terms of war: he would win small victories but then suffer setbacks. "The war is raging anew as violently as before," he wrote. "The enemy ... has burst all the chains

►

Kepler's model of the orbits of the planets, circa 1596. Brahe and Kepler developed the *Rudolphine Tables* on the theory that the planets revolved around the sun in elliptical orbits.

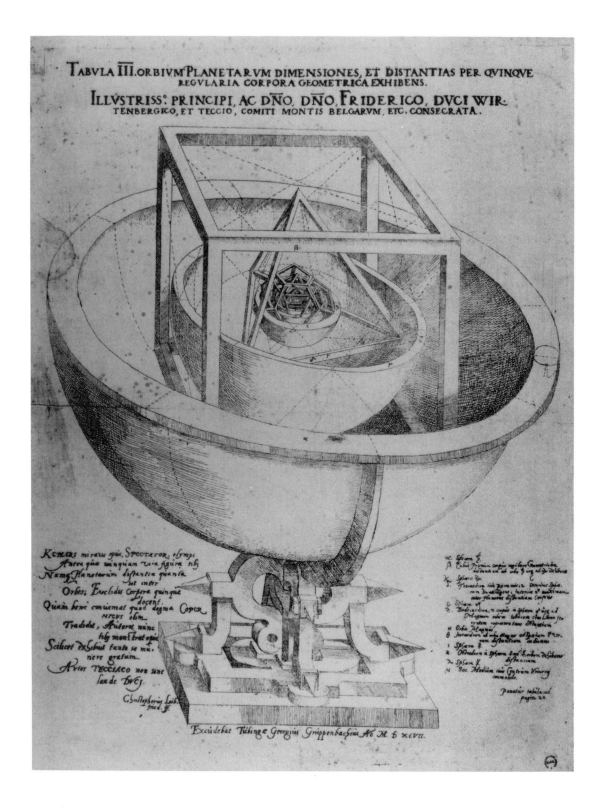

of equations, and broken forth from the prisons of the tables" (Kepler in Lodge, p. 69). After trying hundreds of hypotheses, Kepler finally came up with a brilliant guess that was verified by Brahe's data. The vision of planets moving in ellipses apparently came to Kepler in a dream, and when he awoke, he spent the rest of the night and the next day testing his theory. At last he had discovered the first two laws of planetary motion.

Setbacks and hardship. While Kepler searched for the answers to more questions about the planets, he suffered many hardships in his personal life. By 1611 both his wife and his young son had died. He was left alone to care for his two remaining small children. Kepler's life was further complicated by Emperor Rudolf II's death in 1612. The emperor had been his patron, and after he died, Kepler's salary was cut off. In order to provide for his children, Kepler was forced to leave Benatky and set aside work on Brahe's research.

Third law. Kepler once again became a professor of astronomy, this time at the university in Linz. To make extra money, he published an almanac that predicted future political events and weather patterns. In 1618, after sixteen years of investigation, Kepler finally hit upon his third law.

The Thrill of Discovery

When Kepler discovered his first two laws, he sketched a triumphant goddess figure to the right of his geometric diagram. He was clearly thrilled at his monumental discovery. The first two laws are 1) planets move in ellipses and 2) the radius vector (the line joining the sun and planet) sweeps out equal areas in equal times.

At age forty-seven Kepler had fulfilled his lifelong dream and lived to see it published. However, because his third law was based on the Copernican idea of a sun-centered solar system, his book was banned by the church. (The third law states that the square of the time of each planet's revolution is proportional to the cube of its mean distance from the sun.) The church decree adversely affected his career; he was never able to secure a publisher for his work again.

Aftermath

Tables published. For an entire decade Kepler was unable to publish his own work, so he once again took up the *Rudolphine*

Tables, which Brahe had begun. They were published in 1627, but Kepler had to pay for the printing himself. He had promised Brahe at his death he would see them published and though he was very poor, he fulfilled his great friend's last request.

Death. Unfortunately, Kepler's last years were ones of hardship and struggle. He was owed a considerable amount of money from the Holy Roman Empire and in 1630 traveled to Prague to petition the government for his past-due wages. However, on the trip he became very ill and in November 1630, at age fifty-nine, he died. He was buried at St. Peter's Church in Ratisbon, Germany.

Legacy. Though Kepler struggled during most of his life and saw much of his work banned, he ultimately succeeded in overcoming adversity and revolutionizing astronomy. Kepler served as the interpreter of Brahe's observations, and together their work formed the basis of modern astronomy. His three laws of planetary motion proved the reality of a sun-centered solar system and provided the foundation for Sir Isaac Newton's laws of gravity.

Kepler and Galileo

Kepler and Galileo Galilei, inventor of the telescope, had an especially rich exchange of ideas over the years. Galileo credited Kepler with being the first and practically the only person to have complete faith in Galileo's assertions. In spite of this friendship, Galileo kept some information from Kepler. For example, he once promised Kepler a telescope but never delivered it.

For More Information

Lodge, Oliver. *Pioneers of Science.* London: St. Martin's, 1913.

Ronan, Colin. *The Astronomers.* New York: Hill & Wang, 1964.

Rosen, Edward, editor. *Kepler's Conversation with Galileo's Sidereal Messenger.* New York: Johnson Reprint Corporation, 1965.

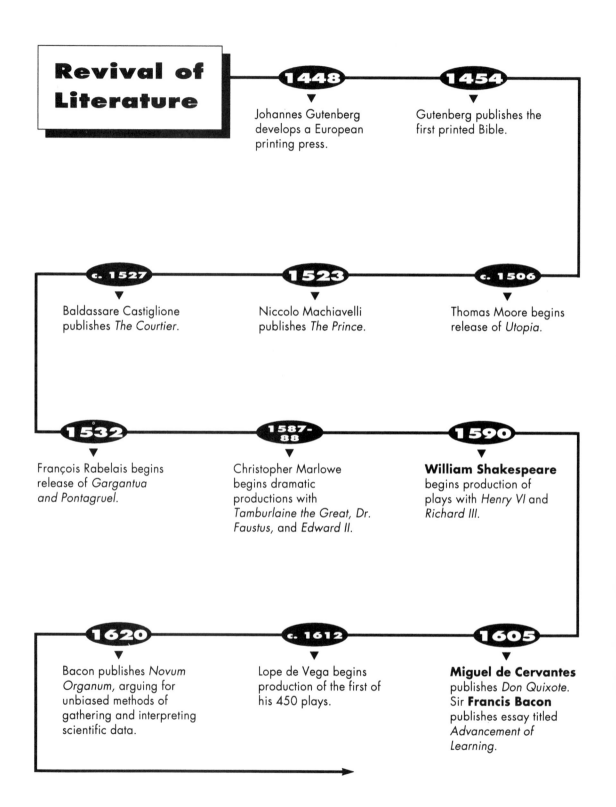

Revival of Literature

1448
Johannes Gutenberg develops a European printing press.

1454
Gutenberg publishes the first printed Bible.

c. 1506
Thomas Moore begins release of *Utopia*.

1523
Niccolo Machiavelli publishes *The Prince*.

c. 1527
Baldassare Castiglione publishes *The Courtier*.

1532
François Rabelais begins release of *Gargantua and Pontagruel*.

1587-88
Christopher Marlowe begins dramatic productions with *Tamburlaine the Great*, *Dr. Faustus*, and *Edward II*.

1590
William Shakespeare begins production of plays with *Henry VI* and *Richard III*.

1605
Miguel de Cervantes publishes *Don Quixote*. Sir **Francis Bacon** publishes essay titled *Advancement of Learning*.

c. 1612
Lope de Vega begins production of the first of his 450 plays.

1620
Bacon publishes *Novum Organum*, arguing for unbiased methods of gathering and interpreting scientific data.

REVIVAL OF LITERATURE

In 1448 Johannes Gutenberg introduced the printing press and movable type to Europe. His invention made books accessible to European readers and helped to accelerate an interest in classical literature that had been growing for more than a hundred years. In 1453 Constantinople fell to the Turks, and its scholars fled to the west, bringing with them Greek and Roman manuscripts. The sudden surge of intellectuals and the revival of ancient literature was part of the uprising in art, science, and literature that is known as the Renaissance.

The new order began with literature and religion in fourteenth-century Italy, when the power of the Roman Catholic Church was severely challenged. For a time, the church was torn and weakened; once there were even two popes—one in France, the other in Rome—dividing the power of the church and clergy. Italian writers Dante Alighieri and Francesco Petrarca (Petrarch) led the Renaissance. In his *Divine Comedy*, Dante exposed Italian tradition to critical examination; Petrarch dreamed of returning to the golden days of early Rome. Along with Giovanni Boccaccio, author of the *Decameron*, Dante and Petrarch guided European writers in exploring the potential of individual thought. This growing "humanistic" movement ran counter to medieval church authority and the domination of feudal rulers.

With the development of the printing press, the infusion of ancient Greek literature from Constantinople, and the exploratory work of the three fourteenth-century writers, a new wave of literature began in Europe. When the Germans conquered both Rome and Florence in 1527, the financing and energy that drove the Italian Renaissance faded. By that time, however, the impulse for newness and excellence in literature, science, and the arts had spread across Europe. Some writers challenged every suggestion of domination by government or religious authority, and others vigorously defended the power of church and state. **William Shakespeare** and Sir **Francis Bacon** were among the poets, novelists, essayists, and dramatists who created a great mass of works that examined the human predicament.

At the same time, civil and religious authority was being challenged throughout Europe. Great city-states such as Florence and Rome turned toward more democratic governments. The old ways were slow to fade, however, and in Spain two writers defied them in new works. **Miguel de Cervantes** mocked old patterns of chivalry in *Don Quixote,* while Lope de Vega inspired his compatriots to examine their own behaviors and beliefs through more than 450 plays. In the fifteenth and sixteenth centuries, the new openness of the Renaissance persisted even as Europe reverted to a system of absolute monarchies.

◄
***The Sack of Rome, 1527,* by Brueghel the Elder; by the time the Germans conquered Rome, the impulse for newness and excellence in literature, science, and the arts had spread across Europe.**

Francis Bacon

1561-1626

Personal Background

Noble birth. Francis Bacon was born into a noble English family on January 22, 1561. His father, Nicholas, was Lord Keeper of the Seal, an honorary post in the court of Queen Elizabeth I, and his mother, Ann, was a well-educated gentlewoman. Francis, his siblings, and six half-brothers and half-sisters from his father's first marriage lived in an ancient mansion, York House, on the bank of the Thames River just outside of London, England.

Education. Bacon was educated in the tradition of the nobility of his day. He learned Latin, Greek, French, grammar, and mathematics in preparation for college. His mother was fluent in five languages and was a great help to him in his studies. It was expected that Bacon would follow in his father's footsteps, taking a position in government or in the church.

Environmental influence. Throughout his childhood, Bacon was surrounded by royalty. Queen Elizabeth I visited his home often and took special notice of him. As a member of the aristocracy living at York House, Bacon had leisure time to enjoy his picturesque surroundings. He played with dogs and hawks, hiked along the banks of the Thames, and explored the fertile countryside, which was filled with woods. Though he suffered from poor health as an adult, Bacon enjoyed the outdoors and

▲ Francis Bacon

Event: Building the foundations of modern arts and sciences.

Role: Through his lectures and essays, Sir Francis Bacon laid the foundation for modern education. An avid supporter of exploration and experimentation, he revolutionized the process of understanding nature.

maintained the deep appreciation of nature and love of exploration he developed as a child.

Discord at Trinity. At age thirteen, Francis and his older brother, Anthony, were sent to Trinity College at Cambridge University. The brothers remained very close throughout their entire lives.

Though a bright young man, Bacon did not do exceedingly well at Trinity. At the time, Cambridge was the center of the Protestant Reformation and college educators taught religious dogma more than anything else. Teachers and church leaders—using the philosophy of Aristotle—fostered a reliance on faith over knowledge and were strongly opposed to independent study, free thought, and free speech. Bacon was deeply upset by his teachers' outlook, which he considered "a philosophy only strong for disputations and contentions, but barren of the production of works for the benefit of the life of man" (Bacon in Bowen, p. 35). He thought that education was the key to progress and discovery, and he opposed those who wanted to dwell in the past—those who thought that all the great minds were already dead and that all truths were already understood. Discontented and argumentative, both Francis and Anthony left Trinity College in 1576 without taking degrees.

France. For the next two and a half years, Bacon lived in France with an ambassador, Sir Amias Paulet. While there, he improved his French and learned about the operations of court and diplomacy. However, he was not very impressed by continental Europe, and when his father died, he jumped at the chance to return to England. He never crossed the English Channel again.

His father's legacy. The death of Nicholas Bacon left Francis without much in the way of property or money. As the youngest of his father's sons, he received only a small income. Relatively poor for the first time in his life, Bacon began studying law in hopes of rising in the government ranks and becoming successful. However, he would have to suffer his share of setbacks before achieving the position he desired.

Clashing objectives. Throughout his life, Bacon struggled with two sets of conflicting ambitions. On the one hand, he wanted power, success, money, and respectability; on the other, he longed to follow intellectual pursuits. He was also torn by a sense of duty and questioned whether it was more important to serve his nation's queen or his own mind. In an effort to satisfy all of his goals, he took a government job and looked forward to the day when he would have enough authority to put his own ideas into practice.

Participation: The Advancement of Knowledge

Birth of a thinker. Bacon studied law from 1579 to 1584. With help from his cousin, a high-ranking government official named Robert Cecil, he was admitted into the bar before his education was complete and was a barrister in London by the time he graduated. But instead of practicing law, Bacon read philosophy and began formulating his own ideas. He was inspired during this period and conceived his idea of "instauration," or reform of learning.

At the end of the sixteenth century, Bacon predicted the beginning of a golden age of learning and scientific achievement. Education to this point was rooted in reading and learning about the past. To a great extent, the church considered exploration and discovery a sin and argued that God would reveal knowledge to his people when they were ready to understand it. But Bacon thought education should be based on "observable facts" that would propel humankind toward new knowledge. He began to voice his opinions in public and proposed the institution of new colleges that practiced hands-on education, where students could experiment and use live models to further their understanding of new subjects.

Unafraid and unrestrained, Bacon continued to speak his mind. He became a member of the Parliament (MP) in 1584 and immediately began to express his views openly to his fellow members, using lofty language and an enormous vocabulary. This coupled with his obvious self-confidence made him seem arrogant to many other MPs, so his ideas were largely dismissed.

First of many conflicts. As a prelude to his first major rift with the queen, Bacon went to work for the Earl of Essex (who was later executed for treason). He wrote pamphlets and composed speeches for the earl, who in turn sought to make him attorney general. But having never even tried a case in court, Bacon was unqualified for the prestigious position. In addition, he had angered the queen a short time earlier by speaking out against her proposal for a new tax. In the end, Bacon's archrival, Edward Coke, landed the job of attorney general. Bitter and disappointed, Bacon set out to get the courtroom experience he needed to advance himself.

Begins writing. After losing bids for the offices of attorney general and solicitor general, Bacon was appointed the queen's "counsel extraordinaire," not a very important position but one he used to promote his ideas. In 1586, at the age of twenty-five, he wrote *Maxims of the Law,* a list of legal proverbs that explained the fundamentals of English common law and how it should be practiced. Though not published for a general audience until after his death, the book was widely read by his colleagues. For the next eleven years, Bacon practiced law, studied privately, and honed his ideas. By age thirty-five, he was writing essays that outlined his philosophy.

Essays. Published in 1597, Bacon's *Essays* became popular and sold well through three editions (1597, 1612, and 1625). In attempting to answer the question, "What is truth?," Bacon notes in his *Essays* the effect that supposed truths have on belief and free will. He argues that "truth ... teacheth that the inquiry of truth ... the knowledge of truth ... and the belief of truth ... is the sovereign good of human nature" (Abrams, p. 1673).

Bacon insisted that humankind should engage in a continual search for knowledge and seek to find truth through observable facts and provable methods. Though not a scientist, he outlined the scientific method, which states that conclusive results are the product of repeated experimentation. His concepts were not widely accepted at the time, but they eventually became the standard on which modern education and science are based.

Bacon's ideas were highly original, and the essay form itself was very unique. The essay—a literary composition written from a personal point of view—had been pioneered by Michel de Montaigne; Bacon's use of it, however, was very different from that of its creator. He wrote eloquently and authoritatively, attempting to prove his theories to an audience the way a lawyer argues a case before a jury.

Ups and downs. Though successful, Bacon's essays did not make him rich. He fell into debt and was jailed at least twice for failure to pay his bills. After Queen Elizabeth's death, Bacon developed a close friendship with her successor, King James I. The next year he was knighted by the new king and began moving up in rank. In 1605 he published *Advancement of Learning.* The next year he married Alice Barnham, a wealthy fourteen-year-old girl. Then, in 1607, he was made solicitor general.

The Adversary

Attorney Edward Coke was Francis Bacon's chief adversary in life. Both competed for the same bride, whom Coke won, and the same jobs, which Coke got. The two men disliked each other and sought at every turn to ruin the other's name. Bacon ultimately won the long-running war by having Coke expelled from government under Charles I.

Glory years. By 1610 Bacon was the leading spokesman for the Crown in Parliament. He was well on his way to achieving the wealth and position he needed to advance his ideas. In 1613 he became attorney general and proposed a massive overhaul of the legal system and English common law, arguing that the purpose of law "is no other than the happiness of its citizens" (Bacon in Bowen, p. 147). Many of his reforms, such as the simplification of laws and elimination of outdated statutes, were put into practice. In 1617 he was granted his father's title, Lord Keeper of the Seal, and as such finally had the power to carry out his own ideas.

Over the next several years, Bacon wrote many works, including his acclaimed fable *New Atlantis* and his treatise concerning the interpretation of nature, *Novum Organum* (or *True Directions.*) He added to his essays, expounded his ideas in Parliament, and sought to establish schools that would teach his new methods. But, at age sixty, Bacon realized he might not live to see his work carried out. "I have ... constructed the machine, though I may not succeed in setting it on work," he said, not realizing that his world was about to come crashing down (Bacon in Bowen, p. 104).

▲ Accused of taking bribes while a judge, Bacon was impeached, fined, barred from Parliament, and imprisoned in the Tower of London for three days.

Aftermath

Impeachment. Just as Bacon was at the height of his success, he was attacked by his old rival, Edward Coke, and accused of taking bribes while a judge. Already physically weak, Bacon collapsed under the weight of the charges and nearly died. He was impeached, fined, and barred from Parliament. In addition to losing his title, he was imprisoned in the Tower of London for three days.

Productive retirement. After being banished from government and exiled to his home in Gorhanbury, Bacon wrote for the last five years of his life. He produced, among other things, a history of the Tudors in England, a book on natural history, many more essays, and a joke book called *Apophthegms*. He also conducted experiments to learn more about the natural world.

Though many of his conclusions were erroneous, his recorded methods have proved invaluable.

Restoration and death. When King James died in 1625, Charles I ascended to the throne and Bacon's name was restored at the court. Charles, a great admirer of Bacon's work, once again made him Lord Keeper of the Seal and invited him to attend the next session of Parliament. By this time, though, Bacon was quite ill. He spent his last days conducting experiments, including testing the use of ice as a preservative for meat. He died of pneumonia on April 9, 1626, and was buried in Hertfordshire alongside his mother.

Legacy. Though under-appreciated during his time, Bacon has come to be known as the father of the modern age. His ideas—especially those on education and the scientific method—have been widely adopted as the basis for modern education. Bacon's large body of work provided entertainment as well as enlightenment. As nineteenth-century British poet Percy Shelley put it: "Lord Bacon was a poet. His language has a sweet and majestic rhythm which satisfies the sense, no less than the almost superhuman wisdom of his philosophy satisfies the intellect" (Shelley in Bowen, p. 231).

For More Information

Abrams, M. H., editor. *The Norton Anthology of English Literature*. 5th ed. Vol. 1. New York: Norton, 1986.

Bowen, Catherine Drinker. *Francis Bacon: The Temper of a Man*. Boston: Little, Brown, 1963.

Eiseley, Loren. *Francis Bacon and the Modern Dilemma*. Lincoln: University of Nebraska Press, 1962.

Miguel de Cervantes

1547-1616

Personal Background

Miguel de Cervantes Saavedra was a man of great optimism and will. Both qualities sustained him during the immense hardships he encountered throughout his life.

Born poor. Cervantes was born to a poor family in 1547 in Alcalá de Henares, a college town outside of Madrid, Spain. His father, Rodrigo, worked as an apothecary (pharmacist) and surgeon—not a well-paying profession at the time—and his mother, Leonor, raised their large family. During his childhood, Cervantes moved with his family to many different cities throughout Spain. In 1563 he settled in Seville with his father and older brothers and sisters. A bustling city where artists thrived, Seville served as a busy port and gateway to the New World (the Americas).

Three years later Cervantes moved again, this time to Castile, and then, at the age of nineteen, settled on his own in Madrid. He had a lifelong love of adventure, and the variety of experiences and diversity of cultures in these various cities sparked his imagination. Much of what he experienced as a child appeared later in his work as a writer.

Education. Cervantes received a basic education despite his family's frequent moves. In Madrid he studied under López de Hoyos, who taught him grammar and composition. Cervantes

▲ **Miguel de Cervantes**

Event: Revival of drama and literature in Europe.

Role: Miguel de Cervantes' novel *Don Quixote* began a new trend in literary realism. The book has inspired a host of literary and dramatic works and remains a timeless classic.

also enjoyed reading—especially poetry—and began writing his own verses. When Queen Isabella and her son, Don Carlos, died, he wrote some of the eulogies included in a book compiled by Hoyos. But despite his moderate success as a writer, Cervantes soon grew restless in Madrid. The thirst for adventure, perhaps a legacy from his childhood, became overwhelming, and he seized his first opportunity to travel and see the world.

Participation: The Revival of Drama and Literature in Europe

In Rome. Cervantes first moved to Rome, the hub of Renaissance activity, at age twenty-two. He was awed by his first sight of the city. Upon entering it, he wrote: "O great, O powerful, O sacred Rome ... I greet thee on my knees, a pilgrim new and humble" (Cervantes in Arbo, p. 32).

The young writer began to work for Guilio Acquaviva Aragon, the Italian prelate (a high ranking clergyman). Acquaviva had heard Cervantes' eulogy to Queen Isabella when he visited Spain and, impressed by the author's talents, became his sponsor. Cervantes dreamed of becoming a famous writer in Rome and returning to Spain as a great success. But Acquaviva had little real work for him, and Cervantes was soon sidetracked from writing.

War and Don Juan. The Turks attacked the Venetian territory of Cypress in 1571. Allied forces under Austrian captain-general Don Juan responded, and a war began in Italy. Cervantes eagerly joined the Spanish *tercios,* companies of soldiers who had become part of the allied force, and fought against the Turks. As part of the first infantry unit, he sailed aboard a naval ship to Messina (in Sicily). There he came face to face with the legendary Don Juan and served under him in the battle of Lepanto, a huge naval victory for the allies. Cervantes is said to have suffered miserably from seasickness, but he fought anyway and was severely wounded in his left hand. Because of the injury, he later referred to himself *el manco deo Lepanto,* "the cripple of Lepanto." Don Juan and the war made a lasting impression on Cervantes.

Capture. When the war ended, Cervantes planned to return to Spain. Because of his involvement in the Lepanto victory and his four years of military service, he was given several letters of recommendation from noblemen and Italian officials.

On his journey home, the ship on which he was sailing was hijacked by Algerian pirates. Because of the letters he was carrying, the bandits assumed that he was from a wealthy family and kidnapped him. For five years they tried to ransom him for a high price, never believing his family's insistence that they were poor and could not afford to meet the demands for payment.

Cervantes rotted in an Algerian prison from age twenty-eight to thirty-three. He tried several times to escape but was never successful. Finally, through the hard work and creativity of his mother and sisters, Cervantes was released in 1580. The women had petitioned the church for five years, arriving daily in their black mourning clothes and begging church officials to intervene on behalf of their son and brother. Their ceaseless efforts finally succeeded when a monk, Fray Juan Gil, paid for Cervantes' release.

1580-87: The lean years. Cervantes returned to Spain and settled first in Valencia, then in Madrid. He fought with the Spanish army against Portugal before taking up writing once again. Cervantes tried to establish a reputation as a playwright, writing twenty or thirty plays in seven years, but he had no success. In 1585 he composed his first pastoral romance, a very common literary form of the time. The first story he sold—for the equivalent of $140—was called *Galatea*. It won him the hand of Catalina de Palacios, the eighteen-year-old girl who inspired the story. When

▲ Title page of the first edition of *Don Quixote*, published in Madrid in 1605.

none of his other works sold, Cervantes was forced to get a job. He became a commissary (also known as a deputy or tax collector) for the royal treasury.

From debt to glory. From 1587 to 1598 Cervantes worked for the treasury and tried unsuccessfully to get his work published. After the birth of his daughter, he fell further and further behind in payment of his bills. He was imprisoned several times for failure to pay debts and lost his job in 1598. It is not clear how he supported his family for the next six years, but during that time he wrote his critical masterpiece, *Don Quixote*. An insightful and realistic novel, full of humor, adventure, and truth, *Don Quixote* continues to influence dramatic and literary works.

Cervantes' Optimism

Cervantes' motto reveals the unwavering optimism that supported him through his prison experience and throughout his life: "After the darkness, I hope for the light" (Cervantes in Arbo, p. 206).

The tale of an aged and dim-sighted but valiant knight named Quixote and his greedy but faithful squire Sancho Panza, the story reflects much of Cervantes' own life. Though the comrades are never successful and meet oppression at every turn, they maintain a positive attitude through it all. Cervantes claimed that through his novel, he wanted to destroy the notions of romance in chivalry. He stated that his major purpose was to:

> introduce a new species of writing that might possibly turn young people into a course of reading different from the pomp and parade of romance writing, and dismissing the improbable and marvelous with which novels generally abound, might tend to promote the cause of religion and virtue. (Cervantes in Bell, p. 202)

Don Quixote was published in 1605 and became an instant popular success. Six editions were printed in the first year of its release, but members of the literary elite of the time continued to

▶

The Innkeeper's Wife and Daughter Taking Care of the Don after Being Beaten and Bruised, **an illustration from** *Don Quixote.* **The tale of the aged and dim-sighted but valiant knight named Quixote reflects much of Cervantes' own life.**

misunderstand and disregard the author's work. In addition, publishers paid him very little for his efforts. Cervantes remained a poor and struggling writer until he secured the patronage of the Count of Lemos in 1610.

Aftermath

Another pitfall. Just as Cervantes was approaching the height of his success, he was once again beset by hardship. After helping a dying man in off the streets of his rough neighborhood, he was accused of murder. Cervantes and his family were held for three days of questioning by authorities and then released. Still, the author's reputation was irreparably damaged. He was forced to move to Madrid and lost his bid to become poet laureate of Spain, a position he had wanted all his life. For the next five years, he existed on the moderate earnings from his novel while working on several short stories and the second part of *Don Quixote*.

The Imposter

Before Cervantes could publish his second part of *Don Quixote,* another writer put out a false text under that name. Alonso Fernandez de Avellanda's book was a poor imitation of the original and most readers recognized it as a fake. However, Cervantes was infuriated by it and, in an effort to show his superiority as an author, worked feverishly on his own Part 2. Some critics feel that the stealing of his idea may have aided Cervantes' own creative efforts.

1610-16. In 1610, with the patronage of the Count of Lemos, Cervantes entered into the most productive period of his professional life, producing such works as *Journey to Parnassus,* an autobiographical narrative poem of thwarted dreams, and part two of *Don Quixote.*

Death and legacy. In April 1616 Cervantes—by now very ill—picked up his pen one last time to bid farewell to the world: "Good-bye, all that is charming, good-bye, wit and gaiety, good-bye, you merry friends, for I am dying, and wishing to see you soon contented in another life!" (Cervantes in Arbo, p. 260).

Miguel de Cervantes died on April 23, 1616. (William Shakespeare died on the same day.) His last work, *Persiles y Sigismunda,* was published after his death. Cervantes' own life has come to symbolize a triumph of the spirit. In a tribute to the author, nineteenth-century American poet William Cullen Bryant remembered his optimism:

As o'er the laughter-moving page
Thy readers, o Cervantes, bend,
What sounds of mirth, through age on age,
From every clime of earth ascend! (Ford, p. 87)

For More Information

Arbo, Sebastian Juan. *Cervantes: The Man and His Time.* New York: Vanguard, 1955.

Bell, Aubrey F. G. *Cervantes.* Norman: University of Oklahoma Press, 1947.

Cannavaggio, Jean. *Cervantes.* New York: Norton, 1990.

Ford, J. D. M. *Main Currents of Spanish Literature.* New York: Henry Holt, 1919.

William Shakespeare

1564-1616

Personal Background

Perfect timing. William Shakespeare was born in the midst of the Elizabethan Age, about a dozen years before the first theater opened in London in 1576. He began his career during the reign of Elizabeth I—one of England's most outstanding politicians and a great patron of the arts—and gained popularity during the last two decades of the sixteenth century after the deaths of London's leading playwrights. With the stage literally to himself and the theater arts avidly supported, he quickly became one of the most prolific and innovative dramatists the world has ever known.

Birth and education. Born on April 23, 1564, in Stratford-on-Avon, a small country town outside of London, William was the eldest of Mary Arden and John Shakespeare's six surviving children. His father worked as a glove-maker and rose through local government ranks, becoming "high bailiff," or mayor, in 1569. Shakespeare presumably worked with his father making gloves and may have accompanied him on official business, which included screening plays before they could be shown in public.

Shakespeare was educated at the King's New School in Stratford, beginning at age seven. His grammar school education was heavily based on memorization, especially of Latin grammar and the classics. It appears that the strong focus on memorization led

▲ **William Shakespeare**

Event: Revival of drama and literature in Europe.

Role: Regarded by some critics as the greatest English writer of all time, William Shakespeare had an enormous influence on the history of theater. The author of more than thirty-seven comedies, tragedies, and history plays, he elevated drama to a new level of artistry and popularity and helped establish theater in London.

to Shakespeare's developing a "fabulous aural memory" (Rowse, p. 38). He retained nearly all that he read and heard and later drew on his vast store of information for his writing.

Shakespeare admired the writings of first-century Roman poet Ovid, whose *Fasti* and *Metamorphoses* inspired much of the young author's work. For example, his second narrative poem, "The Rape of Lucrece," came directly from the *Fasti.* He also read Virgil and Horace, other ancient Latin poets; learned Latin grammar from the text by William Lyly; and studied the classical drama of Terence, Plautus, and Palingenus. Shakespeare's knowledge of history was based on sixteenth-century English writer Raphael Holinshed's *Chronicle of English History,* which may account for some of the errors he includes in his history plays. He also clearly knew Bible stories very well, as evidenced by the many biblical references in his writings.

A country boy at heart. Raised in the rural town of Stratford on the bank of the Avon River, Shakespeare was a country boy and remained so, even though he lived the bulk of his adult life in London. He enjoyed gardening, horseback riding, and archery, but lawn bowling is said to have been his favorite pastime. Shakespeare had a deep appreciation of nature and animals and revealed it when he wrote hunting scenes, usually making them more sympathetic to the stalked animal than to the hunter.

Marriage and London. By 1577 Shakespeare's father had all but abandoned his glove-making business for public life and had gotten himself deeply in debt. Because of this, Shakespeare could not afford to attend college and seems to have worked either as a glove-maker or teacher through age twenty. At eighteen, he married Anne Hathaway, a woman from a respected family who was eight years his senior. In May 1583 their first daughter, Susanna, was born; twins Hamnet and Judith followed in February 1585.

Shortly after the birth of his twins, Shakespeare left his new family in Stratford and ventured to London to pursue his dream of a career in the theater. Whether he joined a touring theater company or went on his own is unclear. One thing is certain: he hit London at the right time, just as theater was beginning to flourish

▲ Under Queen Elizabeth I's rule, people of all classes began attending
the theater, providing a rich and diverse audience that perfectly suited
the talents of Shakespeare.

and actors and playwrights were in demand. Right away he landed
a job in the Lord Admiral's Men theater company, entering as an
actor and reader of new plays. From there he worked his way up
and was fortunate enough to be part of the same company as

115

dramatist Christopher Marlowe, who became both a rival and an adviser.

Participation:
Revival of English Drama and Literature

London in the 1580s. When Shakespeare arrived in London during the reign of Queen Elizabeth, England was just coming into her own as a great imperial power. Pride in the nation was great—especially after the defeat of the Spanish Armada in 1588—and England was establishing herself as a world-class center of the arts. Queen Elizabeth I set the tone. She was not only a master politician but an ardent patron of the arts. Under her rule, people of all classes began attending the theater, providing a rich and diverse audience that perfectly suited the talents of Shakespeare.

Shakespeare was heavily influenced by events going on around him. There were episodes of extreme violence in Britain, such as the beheading of Mary, Queen of Scots, ordered by Elizabeth; bloody rivalries for succession to the throne, such as the Duke of Essex's attempted overthrow of Elizabeth; and great sea battles and excursions, such as the defeat of the Spanish Armada and Sir Francis Drake's circling of the world. All of these incidents provided a wealth of material from which Shakespeare drew and created his greatest masterpieces.

Plague, poetry, and patronage. After working his way up in the Admiral's Men, Shakespeare joined Lord Pembroke's Men. By 1592 he had written *Henry IV Part 1, The Comedy of Errors,* and *The Two Gentlemen of Verona* and was writing for the acting companies of Lords Derby, Sussex, and Pembroke. However, in late 1592 the bubonic plague ravaged London, killing 10 percent of the population. All the theaters in the city were closed and the actors were forced to leave. Shakespeare probably went back to Stratford and began working on his first narrative poem, *Venus and Adonis.*

Shakespeare wanted to establish himself as a serious writer, and he sought to secure a patron. Because he had not attended college like the leading writers of the late sixteenth century in Lon-

▲ **Anne Hathaway Shakespeare; Anne took little part in her husband's
success; in fact, Shakespeare seldom visited her in Stratford—possibly
only once a year.**

don—Christopher Marlowe, Robert Greene, Edmund Spenser,
Thomas Nashe, John Lyly, George Peele, Thomas Lodge, and
Gabriel Harvey—he had trouble gaining access to the literary
market. In an effort to land a publisher, he began writing sonnets
to Henry Wriothesley, Earl of Southampton, who later became his
patron. But Christopher Marlowe was also vying for Southampton's patronage. *Venus and Adonis* was Shakespeare's attempt to
win Southampton's loyalty, and it succeeded. First published in

1593, the poem was an instant and overwhelming success. It was reprinted at least ten times during Shakespeare's lifetime.

Self-educated playwright. Largely self-educated, Shakespeare began to make a name for himself as a playwright in 1594. Marlowe's untimely death in a bar brawl at age twenty-nine—as well as the deaths of Robert Greene, Thomas Kyd, George Peele, and John Lyly—left the stage wide open for Shakespeare. In addition, Southampton gave the young playwright a considerable sum of money that allowed him to support himself while pursuing his literary career. Shakespeare became head playwright with the Lord Chamberlain's Men and wrote four of his most successful plays: *A Midsummer Night's Dream, Love's Labour's Lost, Romeo and Juliet,* and *The Merchant of Venice.* The Chamberlain's Men gave more than thirty-two performances of Shakespeare's work at court that year and established themselves as the leading theater company in London.

The Globe. The year 1594 also marked the founding of the Globe Theatre by Shakespeare and fellow actors from the Chamberlain's Men. The new theater was located across the Thames River from downtown London. With part ownership of the theater and a stake in the company, Shakespeare had security as an artist and control over his work. Though he could have monopolized all the playwriting himself, he generously gave opportunities to up-and-coming writers, such as Ben Jonson. Shakespeare also played minor roles in some productions, including the ghost in *Hamlet* and Adam in *As You Like It.*

Shakespeare's talent. Shakespeare's talent for weaving personal experience with historical events is legendary. An avid reader and expert observer of the world around him, he appar-

---

Shakespeare and Marlowe

While Shakespeare wrote *Venus and Adonis,* Christopher Marlowe worked on *Hero and Leander.* Each was writing his own poem for Southampton in an effort to win his loyal patronage. Shakespeare alludes to this rivalry in Sonnet 77:

O, how I faint when of you [Southampton] I do write
Knowing a better spirit doth use your name
And in the praise thereof spends all his might
To make me tongue-tied, speaking of your fame!

Ironically, both poems became critical masterpieces. Shakespeare apparently won Southampton's patronage because Marlowe died before finishing *Hero and Leander.*

▲ **Shakespeare performing before Queen Elizabeth and her court; the queen took such a liking to the character of Falstaff that Shakespeare put him in another play,** *The Merry Wives of Windsor.*

ently saw both sides of every situation and could describe the life of a king as accurately as that of a shepherd. His ability to relate to all walks of life and create realistic male and female characters made him immensely popular in his day.

Shakespeare's use of language and his ear for dialogue were equally impressive. He became a master of argument and pun—something the Elizabethans loved. His character Jack Falstaff in the 1596 play *Henry IV, Part 1* is considered one of the greatest comedic characters ever created. Queen Elizabeth took such a liking to Falstaff that Shakespeare put him in another play, *The Merry Wives of Windsor,* especially for her.

To tragedies and romances. Through the 1590s and early 1600s, Shakespeare continued to develop as an artist. From 1600 to 1604 he wrote *Hamlet, Troilus and Cressida, All's Well That*

Ends Well, and *Measure for Measure.* By 1608 he had written two of his greatest tragedies, *Othello* and *King Lear,* and the next year he worked on romances, then on his last play, a farewell to the theater called *The Tempest.*

The diverse range of material Shakespeare produced reflects his life and times. By the mid-1590s he was experiencing huge success and was generally regarded as the greatest playwright in London. He incorporated current events into his work, such as the heated debate over aging Queen Elizabeth's successor. He also drew writing ideas from incidents in his personal life, including the tragic deaths of his son and his father within a short span of time around 1595. In addition, the author's later sonnets to a mysterious "dark lady" suggest that he was having an extramarital affair. All these sources helped Shakespeare to produce one of the largest and most varied bodies of work any playwright has ever compiled.

Aftermath

Retirement. In 1609, at the height of his success, Shakespeare purchased the second largest house in Stratford, called New Place. Though primarily retired after 1610, he kept a residence in London and divided his time between country life in Stratford and city life in London. On April 23, 1616, he died in Stratford of an unknown illness at the age of fifty-two. He was buried at Holy Trinity Church under a flagstone that reads:

> Good friend for Jesus' sake forebear
> To dig the dust enclosed here!
> Bless'd be the man that spares these stones
> And curs'd be he that moves my bones.

Rescuing his work. Some debate exists over the authorship of various works credited to Shakespeare. The surviving members of the original Lord Chamberlain's Men, John Heminge and Henry Condell, painstakingly collected and published his First Folio in 1623. Without their effort, the playwright's work may have been lost to the world.

Legacy. Shakespeare is widely regarded as the greatest playwright of all time. Because so little is known of his personal life, he continues to be the subject of heated debate in literary circles. But one universal opinion of his professional life overrides all others: he was a man "to whom all scenes of Europe homage owe. He was not of an age, but for all time!" (Ben Jonson in Abrams, p. 868).

For More Information

Abrams, M. H., editor. *The Norton Anthology of English Literature.* 5th ed. Vol. 1. New York: Norton, 1986.

Bevington, David, editor. *The Complete Works of Shakespeare.* London: Scott, Foresman, 1980.

Ogburn, Charlton. *The Mysterious William Shakespeare.* New York: Dodd, 1984.

Rowse, A. L. *William Shakespeare: A Biography.* New York: Harper, 1963.

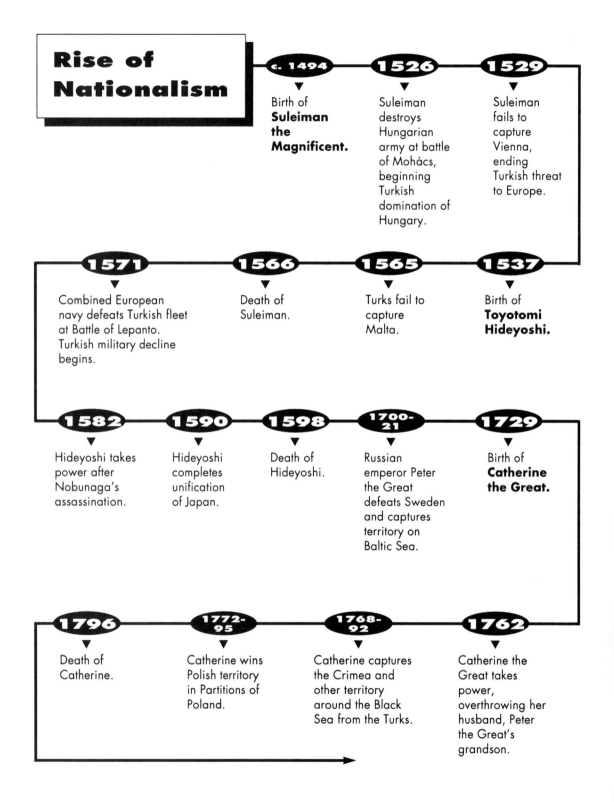

Rise of Nationalism

c. 1494
Birth of **Suleiman the Magnificent.**

1526
Suleiman destroys Hungarian army at battle of Mohács, beginning Turkish domination of Hungary.

1529
Suleiman fails to capture Vienna, ending Turkish threat to Europe.

1571
Combined European navy defeats Turkish fleet at Battle of Lepanto. Turkish military decline begins.

1566
Death of Suleiman.

1565
Turks fail to capture Malta.

1537
Birth of **Toyotomi Hideyoshi.**

1582
Hideyoshi takes power after Nobunaga's assassination.

1590
Hideyoshi completes unification of Japan.

1598
Death of Hideyoshi.

1700-21
Russian emperor Peter the Great defeats Sweden and captures territory on Baltic Sea.

1729
Birth of **Catherine the Great.**

1796
Death of Catherine.

1772-95
Catherine wins Polish territory in Partitions of Poland.

1768-92
Catherine captures the Crimea and other territory around the Black Sea from the Turks.

1762
Catherine the Great takes power, overthrowing her husband, Peter the Great's grandson.

RISE OF NATIONALISM

By the year 1500, at the end of the Middle Ages in Europe, people were beginning to think of nations and boundaries in a new way. The old idea of Christendom—a group of kingdoms held together by their common Christianity—had lost much of its strength. A growing sense of nationalism, fueled by linguistic and cultural differences, took hold on the continent. The feudal monarchies of Christendom soon became the first nation-states of modern Europe, with western European countries such as Spain, Britain, and France leading the way.

In the east, however, centuries of migration and invasion had blurred distinctive cultural boundaries. In areas like Poland, Lithuania, and Ukraine, the Slavic inhabitants spoke languages similar enough to be understood by each other but too different to be considered exactly the same. National unity was hard to forge in such circumstances.

Old-style empires such as those that existed in Rome, Byzantium, and the Holy Roman Empire of Europe in the Middle Ages encompassed many different cultures and kingdoms. Though new nation-states arose and dominated modern history, some old empires held on for centuries. The Ottoman Empire of the Turks offers a good example. Expanding from their base in Anatolia

▲ Japanese battles consisted of individual warriors engaged in hand-to-hand style combat using great samurai swords.

(modern Turkey), the Turks in the fourteenth century built an empire of conquest that included many peoples and cultures. The Ottoman Empire reached its highest point under **Suleiman the Magnificent** in the sixteenth century, expanding west into Europe and east into Mesopotamia. But the powerful empire fell into a slow decline after Suleiman. Within its borders, peoples like the Greeks and the Serbs struggled for national independence in the nineteenth century. Their attempts to found modern nations touched off World War I in 1914, after which the Ottoman Empire was carved up into separate countries.

To the north of the Ottoman Turks, Russia began building an empire under Peter the Great, who conquered territory from Sweden and founded a new capital, St. Petersburg. His successor, **Catherine the Great,** continued Peter's program of imperial conquest by expanding westward into Poland and Ukraine and southward into the Black Sea region of the Crimea.

Empires arose as well in Asia and the Americas. A striking example can be found in Japan—like Britain, also an island—where natural borders helped in forming a strong national identity. Like the kings of Britain, France, and Spain, Japanese rulers unified their feudal lands into a single nation in which cultural borders and political borders were the same. Japan's three unifying rulers—Nobunaga, **Toyotomi Hideyoshi,** and Ieyasu—lived in the 1500s.

Old-style empires were based on conquest; new ones were based largely on domination through trade and commerce, though conquest also continued to play a big role. The European nations established in the Middle Ages took the lead in building these new empires, ushering in the age of world colonialism. Japan, the Asian country whose origins were most like those of Europe's early nations, went on to become the strongest Asian colonial power. In contrast, European nations late to unite, such as Germany and Italy, were also late in building new-style empires of their own.

Suleiman the Magnificent

c. 1494-1566

Personal Background

Suleiman was a descendant of Osman, the fourteenth-century Turkish commander who founded the empire named after him. ("Ottoman" comes from the name Osman.) In the two centuries between the birth of Osman and the birth of Suleiman, Ottoman conquests included all of Anatolia (modern Turkey) and extended westward into the Balkans (modern Romania, Bulgaria, Greece, and the former Yugoslavia).

Line of conquerors. Suleiman thus came from a long line of conquerors, though his father, Selim the Terrible, won more territory in his short reign (1512-1520) than any of their ancestors. Selim conquered Syria, Palestine, and Egypt and made war on the Persian empire to the east. Unlike earlier Ottoman conquerors, he never went to war against Christian armies to the west. Selim left that task to his son, Suleiman.

Unlikely succession. During Suleiman's childhood, it seemed unlikely that either he or his father would ever come to power, for Selim was the youngest of the eight sons of the sultan (or Muslim king). Selim served his father, Bayezid II, as governor of a province on the Black Sea coast, and it is thought that Suleiman's mother, whose name was Haffsa Khatoun, was the daughter of a local chieftain. Suleiman was probably raised in the same region.

▲ **Suleiman the Magnificent**

Event: Expanding the Ottoman Empire.

Role: Sultan of the Turkish Ottoman Empire from 1520 to his death in 1566, Suleiman added Hungary, Mesopotamia (modern Iraq), and parts of the North African coast to the empire's lands. As the Islamic world's most powerful ruler, Suleiman led the Turks many times into battle against Christian European armies. He also gave the Turks a new system of laws, so that while Christians called him "the Magnificent" for his warlike leadership, his own people called him "the Lawgiver."

By the time Suleiman was sixteen, however, only three of Bayezid's sons were still alive: Achmed, the oldest; Korkud, who had no desire to rule; and Selim, Suleiman's father, the youngest. Selim and Achmed were prepared to fight for the succession. Selim, however, had no intention of waiting for Bayezid's death. His bravery and eagerness for battle won him popularity with the army, especially among the sultan's special, first-rate troops, the Janissaries. This group was tired of Bayezid's peaceful ways. Selim overthrew his father early in 1512. He immediately ordered his two brothers to be executed—strangled with a bowstring, the traditional Ottoman method of getting rid of possible rivals to the throne.

Governor. Selim appointed Suleiman governor of Edirne, a major city close to the capital at Istanbul. Over the next eight years, as Selim brought much of the rest of the Muslim world under Ottoman rule, Suleiman served him as a governor, first in Edirne and then in the city of Manissa on the coast of Anatolia. In 1520 Selim the Terrible died of cancer. Confidently and without hesitation, Suleiman stepped into power.

Participation: Expanding the Ottoman Empire

Turning westward. Unlike his father, Suleiman was determined to renew the Turks' attacks on their traditional religious enemies, the Christian kingdoms of Europe. Since the beginning of the Crusades over four centuries earlier, Turks and Europeans had fought against each other. Christian Europeans traditionally saw the Islamic Turks as Christianity's deadly enemy, especially after the Turkish conquest of the Greek Christian city of Constantinople, renamed Istanbul by the Turks. Ottoman expansion brought the empire's borders ever closer to western Europe.

The bloodiest battlefields were in the Balkans, the violent borderland between the Islamic and Christian worlds where Turks had clashed for centuries with Christian Serbs, Hungarians, and others. Several times in the 1400s the Turks attacked the Christian city of Belgrade on the Danube River. Each time, they were defeated by Hungarian or Serbian forces.

Soon after coming to power, Suleiman decided to win revenge for these defeats by capturing Belgrade—and letting the Christian rulers of Europe know that Turkish attention was once again focused on the West.

By land ... In the first two years of his long reign, Suleiman fired the opening shots of what would, for him, be a lifetime of warfare. As the panic-stricken Serbs and Hungarians tried to organize a defense, Suleiman prepared a large army for the attack on Belgrade. In February 1521 he marched north from Istanbul. Capturing other cities as they went, the Turks reached Belgrade in July. The defenders held out for almost two months, but in late August they were finally forced to surrender. Suleiman returned victorious to Istanbul, leaving soldiers and a governor in Belgrade.

... and by sea. The Turks had always been a strong land power. However, despite the fact that he had a relatively weak navy, Suleiman chose to attack the Christians by sea. The days of the Christian Crusader kingdoms in the Holy Land were long over, but one Christian thorn remained in the side of the Islamic world: the island of Rhodes. There, since Crusader times, the Knights of St. John occupied a huge, thick-walled fortress that protected the island's large harbor. From this stronghold close to the Turkish shore, the Knights' powerful ships were able to prevent the Turks from winning control even of their own waters. In early 1522 Suleiman prepared a naval force to capture the island. Meanwhile, the Knights built up their defenses for the oncoming struggle.

Siege of Rhodes. The siege of Rhodes lasted 145 days. Turkish cannons fired thousands of stone balls against the massive walls. Time after time, waves of Turkish soldiers were beaten back. Finally, on December 21, the Knights were forced to give up. Suleiman offered generous terms: the Knights were allowed to leave peacefully in exchange for surrendering Rhodes to the Turks. In only his second year in power, Suleiman had won a second major victory against the forces of Christendom (Christian kingdoms).

Mohács. For the next few years, Suleiman concentrated on getting his government in order, choosing his chief officers and advisers, and creating a new and improved legal system for the

▲ Sixteenth-century Turkish miniature of Suleiman defeating the
Hungarians at Mohács in 1526; the Hungarians lost not only their
army but much of their aristocratic leadership.

empire. Then in 1525 he decided to follow up his victory at Belgrade with a further invasion of Hungary. In April 1526 he set out with his army from Istanbul. When he met the assembled Hungarian forces in August near the town of Mohács, he completely destroyed them. It was another great victory for Suleiman, and a shattering defeat for the Hungarians, who lost not only their army but much of their aristocratic leadership as well. For the next century and a half most of Hungary remained under Ottoman domination. Suleiman, however, pulled his troops back. He did not take direct control of more Hungarian territory—yet.

Instead, he formed an alliance with Prince John Zapolya of Transylvania, one of two men who claimed the Hungarian throne. (The Hungarian king had been killed at Mohács.) Only after John's death in 1540 did Suleiman occupy Hungary directly.

Challenging the Habsburgs. The other claimant to the Hungarian throne was Archduke Ferdinand of Habsburg, younger brother of Charles V, the Holy Roman Emperor. By supporting John, Suleiman challenged the powerful house of Habsburg directly. In the coming decades, through battles on land and on sea, he continued to clash with Charles V, head of the house and Europe's most powerful ruler. As a result, the Ottoman Empire was a key player in European politics for centuries.

> ### A European Ambassador Describes Suleiman
>
> [Suleiman] is thirty-two years old, deadly pale, slender, with an aquiline [eagle-like] nose and a long neck; of no great apparent strength, but his hand is very strong ... and he is said to be able to bend a stiffer bow than anyone else" (Pietro Bragadino, the ambassador from Venice, around the time of the battle of Mohács, in Merriman, pp. 190-91).

Siege of Vienna. Suleiman's contest with Ferdinand over the Hungarian throne soon led to more fighting in Europe. In 1529, three years after Mohács, Suleiman led an army right up to the gates of Vienna, the Austrian capital, besieging the city for several weeks. Four full-scale attacks on the city walls failed, and after heavy losses Suleiman was compelled to withdraw his forces. It was his first real defeat—a turning point not only in his career but also in history, for the fall of Vienna would have left the rest of Europe open to Turkish invasion.

Three years later Suleiman tried again, but a strong defense of the city of Guns (on the way to Vienna) held up his army long enough to make a further advance to Vienna impossible. Europe was safe from a Turkish land attack, though smaller battles continued to take place over the next few decades.

Building a navy. For the next twenty years or so, Suleiman shifted his attention away from the Balkans. Beginning in 1534 he sent his armies against the Persian empire to the east, which had been aggressively expanding its borders. By the following year, Suleiman had added the large area of Mesopotamia, captured from Persia, to his empire.

Suleiman's most ambitious project in these years, however, was building a navy that would allow the Turks to become as powerful at sea as they were on land. To help him, he enlisted one of the most remarkable men of the age, a famous pirate named Khaireddin ("*khayr*-ad-*din*"), known in the West as Barbarossa (or "Red Beard"). From their base on North Africa's Barbary Coast (modern Morocco and Algeria), Barbarossa and other pirates had long preyed upon Christian trading ships. By appointing Barbarossa as his chief naval commander, Suleiman gained control of the Barbary Coast and dominance over the Mediterranean Sea. Meanwhile, lessons learned in the Mediterranean helped Suleiman extend his naval power to the Red Sea and the Persian Gulf, where he had captured territory in his campaigns against Persia.

The power of Roxelana. Like other Muslim rulers, Suleiman had many wives. His favorite was Gulbehar, by whom he had a son, Mustapha. In 1523, however, the sultan's soldiers brought back a captive girl, known as Roxelana, whose charm and sharp sense of humor caught his attention. Clever and ambitious, she became not only his most powerful wife but also an important adviser. By the 1550s they had two sons: Selim and Bayezid. Mustapha, popular and talented, was at one time Suleiman's favorite son; but Roxelana convinced the sultan that Mustapha was plotting against him with the army. Suleiman then ordered his eldest son's execution. Meanwhile, Selim and Bayezid went on to plot against each other, until Selim succeeded in engineering the execution of Bayezid in 1561.

Siege of Malta. In 1565, after several defeats in the Balkans during the 1550s, Suleiman again took on the Knights of St. John. After being driven from Rhodes, the Knights had made their headquarters on the small island of Malta, between Sicily and the North African coast. From this position, they continued to threaten Turkish shipping. Once again, as Suleiman prepared another huge naval force, the Knights strengthened their fortresses on the island. Again the cannonballs flew, but this time, after months of furious fighting and heavy casualties on both sides, the siege failed. When the defeated Turkish naval force returned to Istanbul, the sultan is said to have ordered it to enter the harbor after dark, in an attempt to hide the badly beaten fleet from public view.

Turkish naval power would never again be as strong in the western Mediterranean as it was before the defeat at Malta. Suleiman died the following year, in 1566, while leading his army in battle in Hungary.

Aftermath

Slow decline. Selim, called "the Drunk," succeeded his father but turned out to be better at plotting than at governing. Turkish power had reached its limits under Suleiman. A long, slow decline began after his death. It took hundreds of years, but by the nineteenth century the Ottoman Empire was called "the Sick Man of Europe."

For More Information

Kinross, Lord. *The Ottoman Centuries.* New York: Quill, 1977.

Lamb, Harold. *Suleiman the Magnificent.* Garden City, New York: Doubleday, 1951.

Merriman, Roger Bigelow. *Suleiman the Magnificent.* Cambridge, Massachusetts: Harvard University Press, 1944.

Toyotomi Hideyoshi

1537-1598

Personal Background

Early life. Toyotomi Hideyoshi was born in Nakamura, a village in the province of Owari, Japan. His father was an ordinary soldier. Because of the family's lowly status, there is little record of Hideyoshi's childhood days; apparently he did not attend school or learn to read or write.

Some historians have suggested that Hideyoshi was an ugly child, although paintings of him in later life do not bear that out. However, by the time artists were commissioned to do his portrait, he was the greatest power in Japan and could easily have ordered the painters to make him appear more handsome than he actually was. One famous portrait of Hideyoshi depicts him as having broad shoulders and a large, powerful body. But, according to legend, the Japanese ruler was displeased with the way his face originally appeared in the picture. The artist repainted the face several times until Hideyoshi was content. The finished version—a kindly looking, narrow, and pointed face with a mustache and light beard—was pasted onto the larger, original body, creating an image that appears to have an unusually small head.

Hideyoshi probably had little time for a playful childhood in spite of his lack of school attendance. He was still a young boy when he was taken to groom horses in the stable of Nobunaga Oda. Nobunaga was a nobleman who sought to restore unity to

▲ **Toyotomi Hideyoshi**

Event: The unification of Japan.

Role: One of Japan's strongest rulers, Toyotomi Hideyoshi rose from a stable-hand position to become the greatest general under lord Nobunaga Oda. Taking command of the central government after Nobunaga's death, Hideyoshi continued Nobunaga's work of uniting the local overlords into a single group. He steered Japan into a period of economic prosperity and artistic excellence.

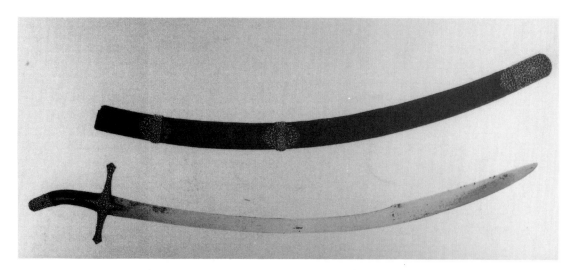

▲ **Samurai sword and scabbard, dating to the mid-sixteenth century; to raise funds, some Japanese Buddhist monks took to making weapons in their monasteries.**

Japan. He gained fame and fought one battle after another with the local feudal noblemen, or overlords, known as *daimyo*. Hideyoshi had many opportunities to hear about battles and to observe the war practices of Nobunaga's soldiers.

Through the ranks. The young groom was a brilliant student of warfare and soon earned promotion to soldier. He fought ably for Nobunaga at a time when Japanese warfare was changing drastically. Until the middle of the fifteenth century, Japanese battles consisted of individual warriors engaged in hand-to-hand style combat using great samurai swords. This type of warfare required considerable skill as a swordsman but little organization of troops.

Trade suddenly brought two changes: the first was the use of spears, which enabled cavalrymen (soldiers on horseback) to bear down on sworded soldiers and dispatch them before coming within sword's reach. The second innovation was the gun. Although explosive powder had been discovered in China, a trading neighbor, guns were not popular until Portuguese sailors arrived in Japan. Nobunaga was quick to take advantage of both these new weapons. Hideyoshi became so adept at using sword, spear, and gun that he made rapid progress through the ranks to become first an officer, then a general in Nobunaga's armies.

Earlier, Buddhism had swept across China and reached Japan. There the old religion took on new forms that attracted the Japanese, and colonies of Buddhist monks grew rapidly. As a result the monks' need for money and land grew as well. To raise funds, some monks had taken to making weapons in their monasteries and hiring themselves out as soldiers to the highest bidder. In a land that was still not strongly bound together under Emperor Nobunaga or a puppet *shogun* (a Japanese military ruler), these monks were threats to the central power.

Nobunaga, then holding a position much like that of a prime minister, hated the Buddhist priests and fought with them at every opportunity. Gathering thirty thousand of his best soldiers, Nobunaga surrounded Hiei, a sacred Japanese mountain where many colonies of Buddhist monks lived. Fearful monks and their followers fled to the top of the mountain. Nobunaga burned their homes and villages, then proceeded to kill off everyone who was found on the mountain. In another battle, he ordered a wall built around twenty thousand men, women, and children, then set fire to the enclosed area, burning all of the people inside.

Lord of Chikazen. Such atrocities were common in the wars of the sixteenth century. Hideyoshi is thought to have taken part in many such battles and garnered much success. In 1575 Nobunaga made him the lord of Chikazen. As a nobleman and landowner, Hideyoshi was entitled to a last name. Nobunaga gave him the name "Hashiba," which he kept until one of Japan's most powerful families, the Fujiwaras, adopted him after his rise to leadership and gave him a new surname, "Toyotomi."

Chief general. Two years after he became lord of Chikazen, Hideyoshi was made chief general of all of Nobunaga's armies. These armies were charged with controlling the *daimyo* some distance from the castle at Kyoto, who were still not completely

Nobunaga and Hideyoshi

The two great dictators of early Japan were equally fine warriors and had some common qualities, but for the most part they were quite different. Nobunaga was a tyrant, described as fierce, heartless, and single-minded. He was so brutal that he killed his own brother to gain control of Japan. Hideyoshi, who could be equally tyrannical, is often described with such words as imaginative, expansive (talkative), and convivial (friendly). He was sometimes seen walking and chatting with servants—particularly with young and nice-looking maids.

▲ An illustration from *Yehon Toyotomi Kunki,* a romance on the life of Hideyoshi by Ryusuitei Tanekiyo, published between 1857 and 1884; it shows a Japanese leader executing three of his soldiers because his advisor suspected them of treason.

ready to obey the central government. In 1577 Hideyoshi was directed to take the army west to subdue twelve overlords in the area of present-day Honshu. Progress was slow, but by 1582 the assignment was nearly completed, and Nobunaga Oda decided that he would personally join the final fighting. On his way to join Hideyoshi, he was killed by enemies within his own army.

Participation: The Unification of Japan

Taking control. Hideyoshi rushed back to Kyoto, where he found that Nobunaga had broken with tradition by making his own son heir to the leadership of Japan. The child was too young to exercise real control over the nation, so regents were appointed to govern for him. Hideyoshi was one of them. He quickly identified the assassins of Nobunaga and had them all killed. Within two years, Hideyoshi had disposed of the other regents and pushed Nobunaga's son aside to become the prime minister of Japan.

His idea was not to be the sole ruler of his nation—only the most important one. The *daimyo* were allowed to keep their control of smaller regions, but Hideyoshi reduced their power. Along with organizing the feudal overlords, he set out to regulate Japan's economy and trade.

Land reform. Hideyoshi supervised a division of Japan's agricultural land, creating a new unit of land measurement, the *koku,* which was the amount of land that would produce a single crop of 180 liters of rice. A *daimyo* had to hold ten thousand *koku* in his own right; Hideyoshi himself owned two million *koku*—more than 10 percent of the nation's total farmland. But he was not the largest landholder: that wealth belonged to Ieyasu Tokugawa.

Ieyasu had been a soldier for a powerful *daimyo* who opposed Nobunaga. When it seemed that Nobunaga was going to achieve victory, Ieyasu became his ally. He rose to become a general just as Hideyoshi had. In the rush to take control when Nobunaga died, Hideyoshi and Ieyasu prepared for battle but later decided that their friendship was too valuable to destroy over a power struggle. To avoid a political conflict, Ieyasu agreed to move away from Kyoto if he could be the wealthiest of the *daimyo;* that is how Ieyasu became the richest landowner in Japan.

Momoyama Period

With the Japanese government and economy under control, Hideyoshi turned his attention to encouraging scholars and artists. A bold new period of artistic development sprang up, producing artworks crafted with gold leaf overlays and brilliant colors, very much in opposition to the delicate landscapes painted before. Hideyoshi's castle was decorated in the new style. Historians call this artistic trend the Momoyama period, naming it after his palace.

Regulating Japan. Hideyoshi adjusted taxes several times so that he could build himself another larger and more beautiful castle. He rapidly put down most of the opposition to his rule and controlled central Japan. When he had all the trade regulations, *daimyo* provinces, and taxes under control, Hideyoshi took one more step to bind the nation to the old feudal system: he banned social advancement. A *daimyo* could not rise in rank. A peasant could not hope to have more land to work and, in fact, no peasant could leave his land or bear arms. These repressive laws actually helped to strengthen the Japanese nation and increase its wealth.

Jesuits and Franciscans. To encourage prosperity and maintain control, Hideyoshi took some drastic measures. Part of Japan's economic success was a result of trade that had been established earlier with the Portuguese. Japanese traders took advantage of the superiority of Portugal's ships, which allowed them to trade with more distant ports. But along with European trade came the influence of Christian missionaries. The first missionaries had arrived in 1549. They were followed about two decades later by members of the Catholic Jesuit order. Nobunaga, in power at the time, accepted the Christians and had even given them land—perhaps to spite the weapon-making Buddhists, whom he viewed as a threat. The Jesuits soon began the process of Christian conversion in Japan; even some of the *daimyo* became Christians.

But after more than 150,000 Japanese had converted to Christianity, Hideyoshi began to worry. In 1587, five years after gaining power, he abruptly ordered all Jesuits out of the country. Sailors from Portugal—a predominantly Catholic country—began to refuse to carry trade goods whenever a Jesuit church was closed, so Hideyoshi quietly failed to enforce his edict. But when another new order of priests, the Franciscans, arrived in Japan, Hideyoshi rounded up the members, had their ears and noses cut off, and then crucified them all.

Hideyoshi then turned his attention to the far north of Japan, where he still had powerful enemies. In 1590 he directed an army of two hundred thousand toward the castle at Odawara, fortress of the enemy Hojo family. After a long siege, the Hojos finally surrendered. The other northerners followed suit, and Hideyoshi was soon in total control of more than one-third of present-day Japan. The country was finally at peace.

Aftermath

Starting a family dynasty. Hideyoshi dreamed of building his own family dynasty but had no son. After he decided to install his nephew as the next ruler in the family, Hideyoshi's wife bore a baby son named Hideyori. In order to suppress any challenge to his son's future reign, Hideyoshi convinced his nephew to commit suicide and then killed off the rest of the nephew's family. Hideyori became heir to the throne. In fact, by 1591 Hideyoshi had given up his position to his son but still controlled Japan as his son's regent.

Ieyasu Tokugawa. Japan was united, prosperity was on the rise, art flourished, and Hideyoshi had guaranteed his family succession in power. Upon the ruler's death in 1598, Ieyasu became regent for Hideyori. Soon Hideyori was pushed aside entirely. Ieyasu Tokugawa took control of Japan, and powerful factions threatened to tear apart the union of the country.

Ieyasu had his castle in Edo (now Tokyo), and his foes were based in Osaka. In 1600 Ieyasu decided to settle with Osaka in an attempt to reunify Japan. Gathering seventy-four thousand troops he met the eighty-two-thousand-soldier army of Osaka at the Battle of Sekigahara ("field of bones"). It was the greatest battle Japan had yet seen. The army of Edo won the battle, forty thousand men of Osaka were killed, and Ieyasu became undisputed ruler of all Japan. He would accomplish what Nobunaga and Hideyoshi could not: the establishment of a family dynasty of Japanese rule—that of the Tokugawa family—that would endure from 1600 to 1867.

For More Information

Dolan, Ronald E., and Robert L. Worlen, editors. *Japan: A Country Study.* Washington, D.C.: Library of Congress, 1992.

Leonard, Jonathan Norton, and the editors of Time-Life Books. *Early Japan.* New York: Time-Life, 1968.

Nish, Ian. *A Short History of Japan.* New York: Praeger, 1968.

Reischauer, Edwin O. *Japan Past and Present.* 3rd ed. New York: Knopf, 1964.

Catherine the Great

1729-1796

Personal Background

The woman the world would know as Catherine II, the Great was born Princess Sophia Augusta Fredericka of Anhalt-Zerbst, on May 2, 1729, in the Pomeranian town of Stettin (now part of Poland). As her title suggests, she was part of Europe's nobility, though her parents were not very high on the social ladder. Her father, Prince Christian August, was a general in the Prussian army, and her mother, Princess Johanna, had relatives in the royal houses of Denmark and Sweden.

Making a match. As a young girl, Sophia enjoyed athletic games more than dolls, and she loved dancing and reading for pleasure much more than studying with her private teachers. She and her mother often visited the palaces of relatives and other members of the European nobility. Princess Johanna hoped to arrange a marriage match for Sophia that would improve the family's social position.

Getting in line. At the age of ten, Sophia first met her eleven-year-old second cousin, Duke Peter Karl Ulrich of Holstein, whose aunt was Empress Elizabeth of Russia (the daughter of Peter the Great, also known as Peter I). Elizabeth, who had no children of her own, chose Peter as her heir. Sophia's cousin was suddenly first in line for one of Europe's most important thrones; Princess Johanna urged Elizabeth to choose Sophia as Peter's wife.

▲ **Catherine the Great**

Event: The expansion of Russia.

Role: Empress Catherine the Great of Russia built on the work of an earlier Russian ruler, Peter the Great, who was her husband's grandfather. During her thirty-four-year reign, Catherine modernized the Russian economy and expanded her country's borders westward into Poland and Ukraine and southward to the Black Sea.

To Russia. Elizabeth had her own reasons for being open to the idea. The most important reason was political: Sophia's family, like Duke Peter's, was closely allied to Prussia, a rising European power close to Russia's borders. So in January 1744, in the cold of the northern winter, fourteen-year-old Sophia set out with her mother by horse-drawn coach on the six-week trip to Russia. Arriving in the Russian capital of Moscow, they were greeted by Elizabeth and Peter, who was then grand duke. The visit went smoothly, though young Peter seemed to Sophia a sickly and rather dull boy.

Catherine. That June, Sophia—who was raised as a Lutheran Protestant—converted to Orthodoxy, the Russian form of Christianity. She also took the Russian name Ekaterina (Catherine), chosen for her by Elizabeth. (The last Sophia in the Russian royal family was Peter the Great's disgraced half-sister, who tried to take power at the beginning of his rule and died in prison. Hence, the name was thought unlucky.) In August of the following year, after several postponements because of Peter's poor health, Catherine married the heir to the Russian throne.

Participation: The Expansion of Russia

Years as a grand duchess. For the next sixteen years, as she grew from a young girl into a mature woman, Catherine lived under the domination of the strong-willed Elizabeth. The marriage to Peter was not a love match; as with other such political marriages, Catherine's main duty was to provide a healthy son who could be Peter's heir. Elizabeth made it clear that she viewed this as Catherine's responsibility, not Peter's. Yet Peter clearly had little interest in sex. His greatest enjoyment seemed to come from dressing up in uniform, practicing sword-fighting, and other "military" pursuits—all of which he did with the approach of a child playing soldiers. Some scholars have even suggested that Peter might have been mildly retarded.

Lovers and an heir. With a high amount of physical energy and, according to some historical sources, a high sex drive to go along with it, Catherine engaged in numerous extramarital affairs.

▲ Peter III; some observers believe that Catherine had ordered her
husband's death—a charge that would hang like a shadow over the
rest of her reign.

Her lovers were usually attached in some way to the Russian
court. Whether by these suitors (as she later claimed) or by Peter,
she became pregnant several times. After two disappointing mis-
carriages, in 1754 she gave birth to a boy. Elizabeth took over
right away, naming him Paul and not even letting Catherine see
him for over a week. A daughter, Anna, born in 1757, died only
two years later; a second son, Alexis, was born in 1762.

145

Succession and overthrow of Peter III. Elizabeth died in December 1761, and Catherine's husband came to the throne as Emperor Peter III. Childish, bad-tempered, and wrapped up in games with the German soldiers he had brought with him from Holstein, Peter had few allies among the Russian nobles. He never even bothered to learn Russian properly, preferring his native German. Catherine, by contrast, embraced the Russian language and culture. In the summer of 1762, a group of nobles led by Aleksei Orlov overthrew Peter. Aleksei's brother Grigori (Catherine's lover at the time) helped plan the overthrow. Having carefully won the army's support beforehand, the nobles immediately proclaimed Catherine ruler in her husband's place.

Murder of Peter. Only a week later, word came that Peter had died in prison during a fight with one of his guards. No one was ever punished for Peter's murder. Some observers believe that Catherine had ordered his death—a charge that would hang like a shadow over the rest of her reign.

Enlightenment ideals... Catherine encountered huge problems at the beginning of her reign, but she faced them with wisdom and confidence. A hungry reader, the new empress had a keen interest in French "Enlightenment" thinkers of the time such as Voltaire. Until his death, in fact, she exchanged enthusiastic letters with Voltaire, the leading figure on the European literary scene in the eighteenth century. Deeply influenced by the modern, democratic theories of such thinkers, she tried early on in her reign to put their ideas into practice. One result was the formation in 1765 of the Free Economic Society, a group of officials and nobles dedicated to the modernization of Russian farming. This and other such programs benefited the nobles and, to a lesser extent, the Russian economy as a whole.

Beginning in 1764, Catherine also personally wrote a collection of laws and guidelines called the *Bolshoi Nakaz* ("Great Instruction"). Two years later she called for selected deputies from all parts of Russia to meet in a convention and redesign Russia's legal code.

... and feudal realities. Bogged down by disputes among the deputies, the convention got nowhere. A major problem was

Russia's system of serfdom, in which peasant farmers (serfs) were tied to the land for life by laws that prevented them from moving. The land, in turn, was owned by nobles, to whom the serfs had to pay rent; this vicious cycle kept the serfs in poverty. Catherine wished to end this carry-over from feudal times but faced harsh opposition from the nobles. On the other hand, she knew that the serfs' grinding poverty could lead to revolts—as it did, for example, between 1773 and 1775, when she faced a widespread serf rebellion led by Yemelian Pugachev. The issue of the serfs would continue to haunt Catherine's successors.

Black Sea coast. Just as Sweden had been Russia's most powerful enemy in the north, Turkey—the old and declining Ottoman Empire—was its largest foe in the south. At the time, Turkish territory included the Balkans (Greece, Bulgaria, Romania, Serbia) and the northern coast of the Black Sea, a waterway that held out the promise of expanded Russian power in the south. The fertile Crimea, with its valuable trading ports, had attracted Russian rulers since before Peter's day. (The Crimea is the peninsula separating the Black Sea from the Sea of Azov.) Even Peter, however, had failed to gain control of these Black Sea lands. The Turks defeated Peter's army in 1711. Catherine knew she could do better.

> ### Russian Expansion Under Peter the Great
>
> One of Peter's main goals was to introduce western ways to Russia, which he did most successfully with his army. When Russian forces were badly defeated by Sweden in 1700, Peter rebuilt them using up-to-date western training and equipment. After Sweden invaded in 1707, Peter shattered the Swedish army at the battle of Poltava. Defeat of powerful Sweden in this "Great Northern War" made Russia into a major European power and gave her control of the valuable Baltic coast.

War with Turkey. In 1768 Russian cossacks—bands of roving warriors on horseback—raided a Crimean town under Turkish rule. Nervous about Russia's plans for domination of the Black Sea, Turkey declared war. It was exactly what Catherine was waiting for. Well trained and organized, the Russian army scored a series of brilliant victories against the Turks. The climax came in June 1770, when Russian ships completely destroyed the Turkish navy at the battle of Chesme in the Aegean Sea. "Russia's first naval victory in nine hundred years," Catherine called it happily in a letter to Voltaire. "They say that the earth and sea trembled with

▲ Russian cossacks battling the Turks; well trained and organized, the Russian army scored a series of brilliant victories against the Turks.

the huge number of exploding ships" (Catherine in Alexander, pp. 132-33). The war ended with the Treaty of Kucuk Kainarji in 1774. Under the treaty, Russia won "independence" for the Crimea, including key ports on the Black Sea and the Sea of Azov and full navigation rights on the Black Sea. Catherine annexed the Crimea in 1783 and made further territorial gains in a second war with Turkey from 1787 to 1792.

Westward expansion. While increasing her influence in the south, Catherine was also moving to expand Russian control of lands to the west: the fertile Ukraine and eastern parts of Poland. Extending north from the western end of the Black Sea, the rich farmlands of Ukraine had been largely occupied by cossacks. Mostly of Russian heritage, the cossacks took many of their nomadic ways from the Mongol conquerors of past centuries. Early in her reign, Catherine brought the unruly cossack leaders in Ukraine under Russian government control.

Then, beginning in 1772, Russia and Prussia—Europe's two rising powers—divided weaker Poland, which lay between them. In three separate "Partitions of Poland" (1772, 1793 and 1795), Russia gained most of Poland east of the city of Warsaw, while Prussia and her ally Austria were given the rest.

Aftermath

The Great. By the end of her reign, Catherine was recognized as one of history's most talented rulers. Even during her lifetime she was called "Catherine the Great," joining the small group of rulers—all men, except for her—known by that title. She died on November 6, 1796, at the age of sixty-seven, from complications of a stroke.

For More Information

Alexander, John T. *Catherine the Great*. New York: Oxford University Press, 1989.

Cronin, Vincent. *Catherine: Empress of All the Russias*. New York: Morrow, 1978.

Erickson, Carrolly. *Great Catherine*. New York: Crown, 1994.

Enlightenment

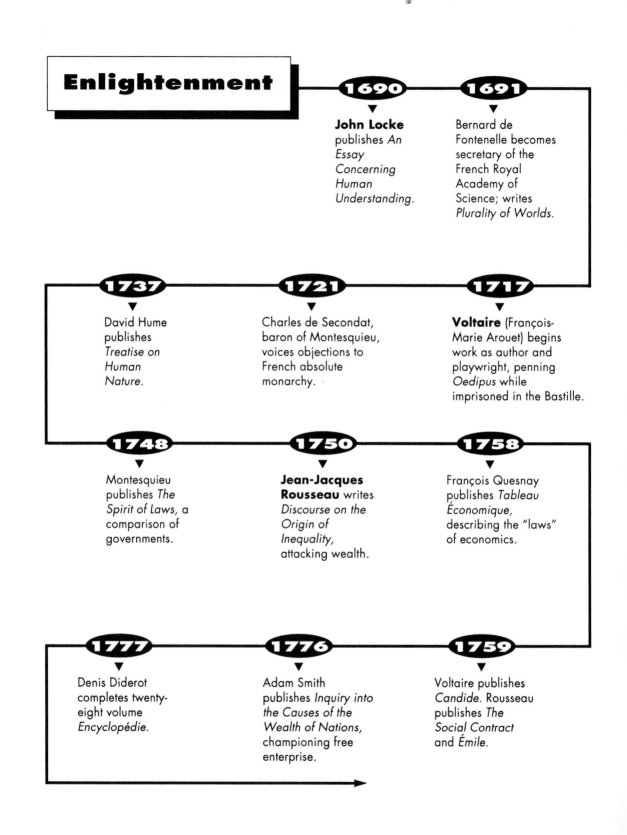

1690
▼
John Locke publishes *An Essay Concerning Human Understanding.*

1691
▼
Bernard de Fontenelle becomes secretary of the French Royal Academy of Science; writes *Plurality of Worlds.*

1737
▼
David Hume publishes *Treatise on Human Nature.*

1721
▼
Charles de Secondat, baron of Montesquieu, voices objections to French absolute monarchy.

1717
▼
Voltaire (François-Marie Arouet) begins work as author and playwright, penning *Oedipus* while imprisoned in the Bastille.

1748
▼
Montesquieu publishes *The Spirit of Laws,* a comparison of governments.

1750
▼
Jean-Jacques Rousseau writes *Discourse on the Origin of Inequality,* attacking wealth.

1758
▼
François Quesnay publishes *Tableau Économique,* describing the "laws" of economics.

1777
▼
Denis Diderot completes twenty-eight volume *Encyclopédie.*

1776
▼
Adam Smith publishes *Inquiry into the Causes of the Wealth of Nations,* championing free enterprise.

1759
▼
Voltaire publishes *Candide.* Rousseau publishes *The Social Contract* and *Émile.*

ENLIGHTENMENT

More than a hundred years after Isaac Newton published his rules of reasoning in *Mathematical Principles of Natural Philosophy*, German philosopher Immanuel Kant stated his motto for the philosophical movement known as the Enlightenment: "Dare to know: have the courage to use your own intelligence!"

Before the end of the 1600s, the old world had been shaken by a scientific revolution during which Copernicus, Galileo, Johannes Kepler, and others drastically changed human perception of the universe. The reliance on direct observation, as opposed to trust in the works of ancient scholars, led to the separation of a branch of philosophy we call science. **John Locke** applied the scientific method to an investigation of human understanding. Bernard de Fontenelle, secretary of the French Royal Academy of Science, worked to popularize the new approach to learning. Newton joined these pioneers in trying to define standard rules for reasoning.

Voltaire. Fresh and innovative ideas sprang up throughout Europe in the eighteenth century. Among them was the notion that humans were capable of discovering truths about almost everything without direction from deities, churches, or governments. The chief spokesman for the idea of individual worth and capability was the French author known as **Voltaire.** On a visit

▲ Jean-Jacques Rousseau contemplates the wild beauties of Switzerland;
during the Enlightenment, efforts were made to present a unified view
of nature.

to England, he was impressed by the degree of individual freedom given to the nation's citizens. That led to the publication of his *Letters Concerning the English Nation* and a lifelong dedication to examining human institutions.

The expansion of science and reason. A wave of scientific investigations and reasoned arguments arose during the 1700s. At the center of a group of intellectuals called *Philosophes* were two men—Denis Diderot, editor of the great eighteenth-century French encyclopedia, and **Jean-Jacques Rousseau,** whose ideas inspired significant political and cultural changes. The *Philosophes* studied such topics as government, marketing, economics, and law enforcement. Individual goals were examined in view of societal needs, and efforts were made to present a unified view of nature.

Challenges of the Enlightenment. Throughout the period known as the Enlightenment, a new emphasis on the power of human reasoning sparked a serious clash with tradition. Religion and faith were cast aside; conclusions were drawn from observations—particularly observations that could be verified by counting and measuring. So radical were some of the approaches of the *Philosophes* that it became dangerous for them to write about and discuss their findings. In the midst of this intellectual growth, women—particularly wealthy women—joined the traditionally male-dominated literary arena. They invested their time and money to maintain "salons," where scholars could gather and exchange their ideas secretly, or at least not so openly as to cause political alarm.

> ### Some Salonkeepers of the Enlightenment
>
> Marie-Thérèse de Geoffrin financed the completion of Diderot's *Encyclopédie.*
>
> The Marquise du Deffand ran a salon frequented by philosophers, writers, and historians such as Montesquieu, Voltaire, and David Hume.
>
> Mademoiselle de Scudéry, herself an author, sheltered many literary figures.
>
> Madame Necker opened her home every Friday for dinner and conversation among the scholars (Spielvogel, pp. 610-11).

Literature and music. During the eighteenth century, the fictional novel gained acceptance as a method of exploring human predicaments. It was also a time of great experimentation in music; George Handel, Johann Sebastian Bach, and Wolfgang Amadeus Mozart were among the era's many innovators.

John Locke

1632-1704

Personal Background

Civil war. John Locke was born August 29, 1632, in the town of Wrington, in Somerset, a county in the south of England. His father, a Puritan and an attorney, was a strict disciplinarian who encouraged young Locke to study and think. England was in the midst of a troubled political period during Locke's childhood. At that time, the nation was ruled by King Charles I, who had placed a tax on ships from seaside towns without the approval of Parliament. Just before Locke's tenth birthday, civil war broke out in England. The war, which would last five years, was fought over the division of power between Parliament and the king. Local judges—forced to collect the unpopular tax—took an active part in the war against Charles. One of them was a friend of Locke's father named Alexander Popham. Thus, politics was always a central topic of discussion in the Locke household.

Judge Popham became a colonel in the Parliamentary army and made Locke's father a captain. For two years both men clashed with the king; later Locke's father returned to his law practice and Popham was elected to Parliament. Through Popham's influence, John Locke was admitted to the prestigious Westminster School in London at the age of fifteen.

Education. Locke attended the Westminster School for five years and received a standard classical education. He endured

▲ John Locke

Event: Writing *An Essay Concerning Human Understanding.*

Role: Locke's liberal essays on philosophy, religion, and politics helped to reform thinking about human abilities. His *Essay Concerning Human Understanding* was an attempt to explain human behavior. Locke sparked considerable controversy with his idea that people were born with a blank tablet (the mind) on which they formed ideas from their own experiences.

long days of tedious study, beginning at five o'clock each morning. The students learned Greek, Latin, Hebrew, and Arabic and memorized the works of the ancient Greek authors. Locke is said to have complained about being forced to learn things he would never use. He often admitted hating school, but he did well enough to win a scholarship to attend Christ Church College at Oxford.

Although Oxford was considered one of the best universities in the world, Locke was disappointed with the school's curriculum. The four-year program in liberal arts required more memorization of ancient texts, an exercise Locke felt was "obscure" and "useless."

Scholasticism. Memorization of the classics began in medieval times. This type of education was based upon the belief that the authority of the ancient Greeks was beyond question—that the ancient Greeks were right about everything. For many centuries, thinkers like Plato, Aristotle, and Hippocrates represented the peak of intellectual achievement in Europe. The Christian philosophers who followed them added the growing body of Christian religious doctrine to the old Greek ideas, creating a vast system of logic, philosophy, and theology known as scholasticism. By the 1650s scholasticism was still the preferred educational method, although its appeal was finally starting to wane.

The Enlightenment. Scholars of the sixteenth and seventeenth centuries—such as French mathematician René Descartes and English writer Sir Francis Bacon—paved the way for a new way of learning. Bacon had even argued that scholasticism should be thrown out altogether in favor of a new system of knowledge based upon observation, experimentation, and measurement.

Although Oxford was still committed to a scholastic-based method of education, the student body in Locke's time contained some of the best minds in Europe, many of whom were rejecting the old ways and turning to experimental science. In fact, three years before Locke arrived at Oxford, some students had started

---

Westminster and the Execution of King Charles

The Westminster School was located near the Whitehall Palace Yard, where King Charles was publicly executed in 1649 after losing the war. Locke may have witnessed the execution, which would explain his later views on the divine right of kings.

---

an experimental philosophy club that held weekly meetings to "test" the truth of classic beliefs using scientific observations. The more experiments they performed, the more apparent it became that much of what they had been taught was wrong. By the time Locke arrived at Oxford in 1652, the club had grown, and Locke soon became a member.

Locke's involvement with the philosophy club increased his interest in medicine. Although his official studies were still entirely classical, he spent much of his time attending medical lectures and performing his own experiments. Eventually, he matched his education with his interests, applying the scientific method to philosophy and theology.

The Royal Society

The experimental philosophy club at Oxford later became the Royal Society, an organization dedicated to promoting the use of experimental science. Locke was formally elected to the Royal Society in 1668.

Locke graduated from Oxford in 1656, began to study for a master's degree, then prepared to study medicine. For a few years, he was a teacher at Oxford and was rumored to have practiced medicine even though he had no degree in the subject. He then became family physician for a British earl, Lord Ashley. A new revolution in England forced the two of them to flee to Holland, and Locke stayed on the European continent until Britain's civil war was over. In 1689 he returned to England, stayed at the Ashley home, took a government job, and began to write essays.

Participation: Writing *An Essay Concerning Human Understanding*

Essayist. Locke wrote essays on many subjects, including religious tolerance, theology, government, and education. Two of his works—one on knowledge and one on political authority—had a particularly profound effect on history. The former, titled *An Essay Concerning Human Understanding,* disputed the scholastic belief in inherited knowledge, while the latter, *Two Treatises of Civil Government,* argued against the notion that a monarch's rule is a God-given right. Both works were published in the same year, 1690, and had a lasting effect on future studies of philosophy, psychology, political science, and religion.

157

By applying scientific principles to the question of how people learn and understand, Locke arrived at a powerful theory that opposed some of the old scholastic ideas. Even so, his theory was not radically new; Christian theologian Thomas Aquinas offered similar ideas on knowledge four hundred years earlier. But Locke's theory was supported so thoroughly by observation and example that seventeenth-century philosophers found it impossible to ignore.

Empiricism. Locke was an empiricist. He believed that all knowledge comes from personal observations and sense experiences: what is seen, heard, tasted, smelled, and touched. This "raw stuff" is then processed and assembled into ideas by the human brain. The notion that the human mind at birth is like a *tabula rosa*, a blank sheet of paper empty of all knowledge, contradicted the widely held view that some knowledge is innate. Locke expounded on this theory in *An Essay Concerning Human Understanding:*

> Let us then suppose the mind to be, as we say, white paper, void of all characters, without any ideas. How comes it to be furnished? Whence comes it by that fast store which the busy and boundless fancy of man has painted on it with an almost endless variety?... Our observation, employed either about external sensible objects or about the internal operations of our mind perceived and reflected on by ourselves, is that which supplies our understanding with all the materials of thinking.

As far back as Plato's time, philosophers generally felt that people were born knowing certain things, such as basic principles of morality and the idea of a God. Locke did not ask his readers to assume the truth of what he wrote; instead, he dared them to prove him wrong by collecting their own data.

Locke on the right of government to rule. Locke's treatises on government sparked additional controversy. Earlier political thinkers claimed that monarchs had a divine right to rule over their subjects. In their view, the absolute right to rule began with the first man, Adam, who had been given authority over all the earth. Locke felt that this interpretation of Biblical law was erroneous and further argued that it would be impossible to trace anyone's lineage back to Adam. He also pointed out that royal families throughout history often contested the throne, and the winner was almost always the one with the biggest army.

Aftermath

Fear and acclaim. Locke wrote his essays in secret and went to extraordinary lengths to keep his life's work hidden. He invented his own private style of shorthand that no one else could read and at times wrote in invisible ink. He never published any of his work until 1689, when he was fifty-seven years old. Over the four years that followed, he published all of his essays, many of them anonymously. He feared for his life at a time when proponents of new ideas were viewed as a threat to the existing government and often punished by death.

Locke's ideas were better received in mainland Europe than in his own country, where people continued to look upon him as a dangerous subversive. He retired from public life in 1700 but continued to write until his death. He was busy working on a series of Biblical commentaries when he died in 1704, at the age of seventy-two.

Effects of his writings. *Two Treatises of Civil Government* had an enormous effect on the politics of the next century. Locke's idea about governments—mainly that they can only exist with the consent of the people—eventually sowed the seeds for the American Revolution. The American Declaration of Independence and the U.S. Constitution are based on principles set forth in Locke's essay.

Locke's Argument Against Divine Right to Rule

In order to make his argument against the concept of "divine right" convincing, Locke tried to apply reason. Suppose, he argued, that the reigning monarch were a queen and that she married one of her subjects. Ancient beliefs held that husbands had absolute power over their wives, so the queen would have to obey her husband. Under the divine right of monarchs, however, she would have absolute power over her husband. It was a clear conflict of old beliefs; Locke claimed that one or the other had to be wrong.

For More Information

Locke, John. *A Letter Concerning Toleration.* Chicago: Encyclopedia Britannica, 1990.

Locke, John. *An Essay Concerning Human Understanding.* New York: Dutton, 1959.

Squadrito, Kathleen. *John Locke.* Boston: Twayne, 1979.

Yolton, John. *John Locke: An Introduction.* New York: Basil Blackwell, 1985.

Voltaire

1694-1778

Personal Background

Early life and education. Voltaire was born François-Marie Arouet on November 21, 1694, to an upper middle-class Parisian family. At birth he was a weak child whose parents held little hope for his survival. But, under the care of a nurse, he gained his strength and within two years became a healthy and mischievous boy.

Voltaire's father was a successful notary whose clients were generally rich and aristocratic. Young Voltaire grew up surrounded by wealthy, influential people who were of a higher social class than his own. Still, he had no trouble impressing everyone with his brightness and comic antics. Even at a very early age, he loved being the center of attention. He first displayed his poetic gifts as a small child.

When Voltaire was ten, he was sent to an exclusive Jesuit school for boys, where he quickly gained a reputation as a class clown. Although he loved learning, he was very resentful of authority and constantly argued with his teachers over religion. The Jesuits—members of the most scholarly order of Catholic priests—taught philosophy rooted in Catholic doctrines. During his seven years at the school, Voltaire became increasingly anti-Catholic. He strongly believed in God and in moral responsibility but denied religious authority and divine revelation. Instead, his beliefs were

▲ Voltaire

Event: Advancing Enlightenment ideals through literature.

Role: A French author of both fiction and nonfiction, Voltaire attacked the beliefs of his time. His most famous work, a short novel titled *Candide,* challenged the premise that "this is the best of all possible worlds." Voltaire was frequently imprisoned and forced to live in exile because of his political beliefs, and many of his books were banned. Nevertheless, he became a champion of Enlightenment thinking and a national hero within his lifetime.

based on purely rational grounds. Voltaire's philosophy, known as *deism,* asserts that God created the world but does not directly involve himself with it. Because it rejects the idea of divine intervention in any form, *deism* contradicts the most basic tenet of Christianity—the belief that God lived on earth as Jesus Christ.

Voltaire the writer. In addition to his startling views on religion, Voltaire had a fondness for writing shockingly scandalous poems and stories. Upon his graduation, he announced to his father that he intended to be a writer. His father thought that literary pursuits were useless and encouraged him to become a lawyer instead. Voltaire reluctantly agreed but spent the next couple of years as a jobless carouser—and wrote in his spare time.

In 1713, when Voltaire was nineteen, his godfather's brother was named the French ambassador to The Hague, in Holland. Complying with his father's wishes, Voltaire went along as the ambassador's page, a nonpaying job. In The Hague, he fell in love and planned to elope, but the ambassador discovered the scheme and sent Voltaire back home in disgrace.

Again, his father pushed him into a legal career, getting him a job as a law clerk, but Voltaire was increasingly drawn into high society and determined to make writing his profession. His friends from school were by then the influential young men of Paris, and through them he was becoming a popular local figure, known for writing poems and plays that poked fun at everything and anyone of importance.

Voltaire in prison. In 1715, just as Voltaire's celebrity status was starting to rise, King Louis XIV died. His successor, Louis XV, was only five years old at the time, so for a while France was ruled by a regent, the Duke of Orléans. The duke was a man of questionable morals, and rumors about him soon began to circulate around Paris. When an anonymous poem surfaced in 1717 accusing the duke of committing incest with his daughter, there was little doubt about its author. The duke imprisoned Voltaire in France's most famous prison, the Bastille, for a year. He was released in the spring of 1718, under the condition that he would not live in Paris. This was Voltaire's first taste of exile, a form of punishment he would receive throughout his life.

▲ The Bastille; when an anonymous poem surfaced in 1717 accusing the Duke of Orléans of committing incest with his daughter, the duke imprisoned Voltaire in the Bastille for a year.

Voltaire stayed at his father's country house in Chatenay through the summer but longed to return to Paris. Meanwhile, a theater company accepted his first play, *Oedipus,* and he began commuting to Paris to oversee the production. (By the time *Oedipus* opened in Paris, he had officially changed his name from Arouet to Voltaire.)

Oedipus was a tremendous success, playing to twenty-seven thousand spectators over a forty-two-night run. By the age of twenty-four, the notorious Voltaire had become a literary sensation.

Participation: Writing for the Enlightenment

Writing diversity. For the rest of his life, Voltaire worked tirelessly, writing plays, poems, novels, history books, philosophy

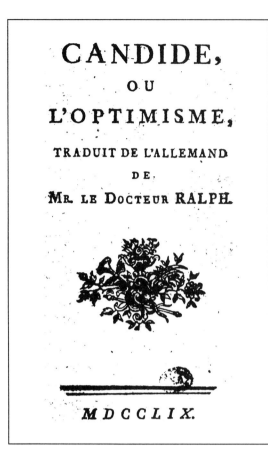

CANDIDE,

O U

L'OPTIMISME,

TRADUIT DE L'ALLEMAND

D E,

MR. LE DOCTEUR RALPH.

MDCCLIX.

▲ Title page of the first edition of *Candide,* published in Geneva in 1759; the short novel challenges the premise that "this is the best of all possible worlds."

texts, encyclopedia articles, and an endless list of pamphlets and letters. Through his works he became known as the chief advocate of the Enlightenment, a philosophical movement rooted in the powers of human reason.

Voltaire did not invent the Enlightenment; most of the views he preached had already been expressed by others. But Voltaire is regarded as a key Enlightenment thinker because—more than anyone else in his time—he helped to popularize the new philosophy in France and abroad. By exploiting every media that existed in his day, Voltaire bombarded European culture with endless assaults against the status quo: Christianity and government practices were his primary targets. Voltaire's writings were distinctive and easily recognizable. Still, most were published anonymously, due to the constant threat of imprisonment the author faced.

Candide. Heavily influenced by the writings of John Locke, Voltaire approached the study of history with an Enlightenment theme. He viewed the evolution of history as the gradual victory of rationalism over ignorance and superstition. This theme also provided the basis for many of his fictional works, most notably *Candide.*

By most standards, *Candide* is not considered a great novel. The plot is unbelievable, and its characters lack depth. Nevertheless, it is the most famous and widely read work by Voltaire. *Candide* is the story of a boy (the title character) who leads a sheltered, idyllic life in a Westphalian castle owned by a powerful lord. When he makes romantic advances toward the lord's daughter, Cunegund, he is immediately banished from the castle and sent into the real world. As the story progresses, Candide and his companion, Pangloss, endure one catastrophe after another. Having witnessed natural disasters, barbarism, and misery in all corners of the globe, Candide comes to the conclusion that the world is plainly insane.

In *Candide,* Voltaire critiques virtually every social and political system of his day. By exaggerating the extremes of human suffering, he demonstrates the hypocrisy of the self-righteous. Most of all, however, his novel stands as an all-out attack on the philosophy of *optimism,* which states that everything that happens—no matter how horrible—is for the best. In its place, Voltaire offers a simple, practical solution to the world's problems: cooperation.

Reactions to the book. *Candide* was written in 1758, when Voltaire was exiled in Geneva, and published anonymously the following year. Voltaire consistently denied that he was the book's author and even called it a "schoolboy's joke." Although *Candide* was banned in Geneva and ordered destroyed, it was immensely popular and contributed to the demise of optimism as a serious philosophy.

Optimism. Optimism was the last defense against the attacks of John Locke. Locke had argued that the divine right of monarchs was absurd, in part because the succession of monarchs was often determined by chance historical factors. Proponents of the belief in divine right maintained that God himself decided the true birthright lineage of rulers by directly controlling history. (In other words, the fact that a particular person rules is proof of God's will that he or she should rule.) This type of thinking leads to the conclusion that all events are destined by God to create the best results; such is the basis of optimism.

Voltaire staunchly opposed the apathy encouraged by optimism. Optimists saw no need to change the world because they believed that it was already "the best of all possible worlds." But Voltaire saw the possibility for progress and improvement as a moral obligation. His own experiences with the injustice of

---

Humorous Voltaire

Voltaire was always joking, even about the most serious subjects. When *Oedipus* became a hit, he was presented with a pension by the same ruler who had imprisoned him in the Bastille. He thanked the duke for buying his meals, but added that, in the future, he would prefer to look after his own lodging.

absolute power no doubt contributed to his opinions. He had been imprisoned—not once, but twice—at a ruler's whim. His first confinement, for a year, was over a poem he wrote. His second term in prison, for a couple of weeks, was due to a quarrel he had with a young nobleman. In neither instance was he given a trial or allowed to produce a defense. For the rest of his life, he was forced to live in perpetual exile, moving from one city to another to avoid imprisonment or death.

Aftermath

Years at Ferney. In the mid-1700s Voltaire served as a royal historiographer. After quarreling with Prussia's King Frederick in 1751, he distanced himself from the monarchy and lived at Ferney on the shore of Lake Geneva off and on. Having accumulated considerable wealth through wise investment, Voltaire added to his money by building a watchmaking industry in competition with the Swiss manufacturers.

While living at Ferney, Voltaire also adopted a noble but poor girl whom he called "Belle et Bonne" ("beautiful and good"). She later became the Marquise de Villete. During her time with Voltaire, she served as an important source of encouragement and helped to make the last twenty years of his life the most productive ever. Much of his writing from that time championed the rights of individuals who had been mistreated.

Death of a hero. In 1778, after a lifetime of exile, Voltaire finally returned to Paris to see the production of his last play, *Irene.* He was given a hero's welcome and spent his final days receiving guests from around the world, including Benjamin Franklin. He died on May 30 of that year, having lived long enough to see the first political outcome of the Enlightenment— the American Revolution. On his deathbed, he asked for paper and ink, with which he wrote: "I die adoring God, loving my

> ### Voltaire on Record
>
> "Atheism and fanaticism are two monsters which may tear society in pieces; but the atheist preserves his reason, which checks his propensity to mischief, while the fanatic is under the influence of madness which is constantly goading him on.
>
> "If you are desirous to prevent the overrunning of a state by any sect, show it toleration" (Voltaire, p. 52).

friends, not hating my enemies, and detesting superstition" (Voltaire in Horne, p. 98).

For More Information

Andrews, Wayne. *Voltaire*. New York: New Directions, 1981.

Bottiglia, William F. *Voltaire: A Collection of Critical Essays*. Englewood Cliffs, New Jersey: Prentice-Hall, 1968.

Horne, Charles F. *Great Men and Famous Women*. New York: Selmar Hess, 1894.

Voltaire. *The Portable Voltaire*. Edited by Ben Ray Redman. New York: Viking, 1968.

Jean-Jacques Rousseau

1712-1778

Personal Background

Geneva. In the early 1700s Geneva, Switzerland, was an independent, walled city. It had a population of about twenty thousand—mostly exiles from France who were seeking more freedom. The people of Geneva were divided across economic and political lines. Wealthy members of the town lived in fine houses on the hill above Lake Geneva, while the poorer workers lived in cheap housing on the flats nearer the water. Although conceived as a democracy on the old Greek style, the Genevan government was actually run by the wealthy few.

Isaac Rousseau. One of the Huguenots (French Protestants) who had settled in the flats of Geneva was a young businessman named Isaac Rousseau. He was a restless man who made his living as a watchmaker but enjoyed dancing and playing the violin.

Rousseau married Susanne Bernard, a beautiful young aristocrat with an adventurous streak. (Several times Susanne found herself in trouble with church authorities—once when she was caught dressed in men's clothing so that she could sneak into a local theater to see a traveling show.) One of Susanne's uncles gave the couple a home on the hill. There they set up housekeeping, and shortly thereafter their first son, François, was born.

Istanbul. Isaac Rousseau apparently grew tired of his small family and equally small business. While François was still young,

▲ **Jean-Jacques Rousseau**

Event: Defining government in the Enlightenment.

Role: Eighteenth-century French philosopher and author Jean-Jacques Rousseau is widely regarded as the father of the French Revolution. He wrote *Discourse on the Origin of Inequality* and *The Social Contract,* which helped to define the human state and the need for government. His views on religion and science brought him into direct confrontation with Voltaire and other writers of the time.

he left his son, wife, and home to sail to Istanbul; he had heard that an increase in trade there had opened up a wealth of business opportunities. A year passed, and then two, and Rousseau did not return. Meanwhile, his wife turned all of her attention to their small son.

The loss of a parent. Isaac finally did return home, and soon he and Susanne had another son, Jean-Jacques. Within a week of the baby's birth, Susanne died of a fever, leaving Isaac to raise the two boys. Historians suggest that Isaac's long stay in Istanbul put a strain on his relationship with his first son. As a result, Isaac gave most of his time and love to Jean-Jacques.

Isaac's final departure. Isaac and Jean-Jacques were inseparable, but Isaac's fierce temper sometimes led to violent episodes. One of Rousseau's earliest memories was of throwing himself between his older brother and his out-of-control father to take a harsh beating upon himself. But, in spite of the changeable behavior of his father and the difficulties with his brother, early life for Jean-Jacques Rousseau was good. His father loved him, and he was surrounded by relatives. In fact, while his father was at work, Rousseau was raised by his aunt Theodora and her eighteen-year-old servant, whom he called *ma mie Jacqueline*.

Some of Rousseau's Major Writings

Discourse on the Sciences and the Arts, 1750

Discourse on the Origin of Inequality, 1750

Letters to Voltaire, 1759

La Nouvelle Héloïse (*The New Eloise*), 1761

The Social Contract, 1762

Émile, 1762

Dictionary of Music, 1767

Confessions, 1782-89

But the tranquil life of reading, enjoying the nature around Geneva, and being pampered came to an abrupt end when Rousseau reached the age of ten. Once more, it was his father's temper that caused the trouble. Isaac fled Geneva over a legal dispute with a wealthy landowner. Eventually, he married again and lived in comfort in another city on the income from Susanne's home.

Still under the care of his aunts and uncles, Jean-Jacques Rousseau was sent to a country school and later apprenticed to an engraver. He felt as though he had been abandoned by his father and tried to escape from the harsh realities of life by losing himself in literature.

Leaving Geneva. Rousseau left the walled city of Geneva in 1741. He set out to walk over the Alps to a town called Amercy, but on the way he was robbed of all his possessions. Rousseau received food and shelter from the Catholic Church, but still his life was desperate.

For many years, Rousseau led a restless life, living on and off at the home of a woman named Madame de Warens and traveling throughout Europe. He eventually made his way to Paris in the hopes of earning a living as a writer. There he met rising French writer and philosopher Denis Diderot. He also met a servant woman named Thérèse Le Vasseur, and the couple began a fifteen-year-long relationship. Together they had five children, but Rousseau placed all of them in an orphanage shortly after their births.

Rousseau's Proposal

When he met and fell in love with Thérèse Le Vasseur, Rousseau was bluntly honest: he promised he would always stay with her but would never marry her. She was equally honest, confessing to having had an affair before they met. Rousseau passed this confession off by recognizing the sexual mores of his day. He apparently claimed that no one could expect to find a twenty-year-old virgin in eighteenth-century Paris.

Participation:
Defining Government in the Enlightenment

Essayist. Through Diderot, Rousseau developed an interest in philosophy and government. He had been hired by Diderot to write entries, mostly on music, for an encyclopedia. In 1749 he entered an essay contest. The topic was the impact of artistic and scientific advancement on morality. His prize-winning essay was later published as *Discourse on the Sciences and the Arts*. The victory and the publication gave Rousseau immediate fame, but his views angered the heroes of the Enlightenment.

Discourse on the Origin of Inequality. In a second essay, titled *Discourse on the Origin of Inequality,* Rousseau wrote about the history of humans, tracing how people had corrupted their lives with material desires. The discourse presents government as an evil but necessary method of organizing human life.

▲ *The Women's March to Versailles* during the French Revolution; Rousseau's themes of liberty and equality put forth in *Émile* soon became the mottoes of the revolution.

Like much of Rousseau's writings, *The Origin of Inequality* uses coarse, even crude, examples to convey the author's ideas. His earthy approach was one tactic that made him at once loved and hated as a writer.

The Social Contract. Rousseau expounded upon his ideas on government in a book titled *The Social Contract.* In it, he reasons that people forfeit some of their freedom in order to have a government that will protect their property. But Rousseau's concept of democracy left the major decisions in the hands of a select few. Still, his book is considered a major influence on revolutionary thought in France.

Émile. A third famous writing by Rousseau, the novel *Émile, or On Education,* tells the story of a young student and his master—a sort of symbolic human-God relationship. The book suggests radical changes in education from the rote memorization of his time.

Aftermath

A troubled soul all his life, Rousseau decided in his later years that the search for material wealth was not the best of goals. For the last fifteen years of his life, he lived in isolation and near insanity. At the same time, he tried to explain himself and his actions by writing his autobiography, *Confessions*. In it, he tries to remember many details of his life but warns that his memory may be faulty. And, according to some critics, many tales in his *Confessions* are indeed fabrications.

Influence. Rousseau's ideas became famous after his death, when revolutionaries in France took up his ideas about the evils of government. They used *Émile* to study the best ways to reform education and tried to achieve a balance between religious tradition and the advancement of the arts and sciences. The themes of liberty and equality soon became the mottoes of the French Revolution.

For More Information

Cranston, Maurice. *Jean-Jacques: The Early Life and Work of Jean-Jacques Rousseau.* New York: Norton, 1982.

Cranston, Maurice. *The Noble Savage.* Chicago: University of Chicago Press, 1991.

Crocker, Lester G. *Jean-Jacques Rousseau: The Quest, 1712-1758.* New York: Macmillan, 1968.

Rousseau, Jean-Jacques. *The Social Contract and Discourses.* Translated by G. D. H. Cole. New York: Dutton, 1950.

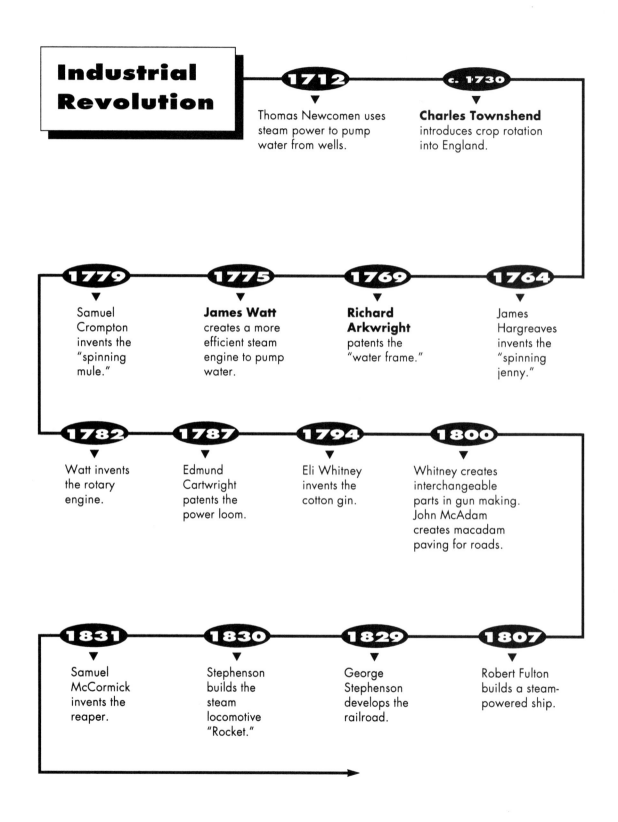

Industrial Revolution

1712
▼
Thomas Newcomen uses steam power to pump water from wells.

c. 1730
▼
Charles Townshend introduces crop rotation into England.

1779
▼
Samuel Crompton invents the "spinning mule."

1775
▼
James Watt creates a more efficient steam engine to pump water.

1769
▼
Richard Arkwright patents the "water frame."

1764
▼
James Hargreaves invents the "spinning jenny."

1782
▼
Watt invents the rotary engine.

1787
▼
Edmund Cartwright patents the power loom.

1794
▼
Eli Whitney invents the cotton gin.

1800
▼
Whitney creates interchangeable parts in gun making. John McAdam creates macadam paving for roads.

1831
▼
Samuel McCormick invents the reaper.

1830
▼
Stephenson builds the steam locomotive "Rocket."

1829
▼
George Stephenson develops the railroad.

1807
▼
Robert Fulton builds a steam-powered ship.

INDUSTRIAL REVOLUTION

The Industrial Revolution began in eighteenth-century Great Britain with the introduction of mechanized production methods. It signaled a radical economic change in the nations of Europe. For centuries people had searched for relief from the painstaking labor involved in the manual production of goods. Power sources like wind and water had been used since the Middle Ages, but the changes of the eighteenth and nineteenth centuries were dramatic by comparison and completely revolutionary.

Pre-revolutionary conditions. Several conditions existed in Britain by the 1700s that set the stage for the revolution. First the production of food and raw materials had become more efficient, leaving a large labor force available to do other work. Innovative individuals worked to develop new machines that would further accelerate the production process. Finally, people with financial resources began to express an interest in investing in these new ventures to add to their profits.

Britain is known for its mineral resources, particularly coal and iron. Its island geography made it a bustling center of international trade in the eighteenth century. England's wealth was a natural outgrowth of the favorable business climate set by the nation's government. The national bank of England financed the building of factories and machines, and a ready market existed both overseas and at home for the array of new products that could be mass-produced by machine power.

Charles Townshend, Sir **Richard Arkwright,** and **James Watt** played key roles in the emergence of the Industrial Revolution by improving on existing ideas for new methods of production. In their day, British landowners generally clung to the old farm methods, using serfs and sharecroppers who were willing to pay to farm small sections of land.

Agricultural advancements. An agricultural revolution was necessary before an industrial revolution could take place. As early as the mid-1600s, English travelers had learned about growing turnips to renew the land after heavy grain planting. But it was Charles Townshend who reorganized his land into larger, more workable tracts and contracted with his lessees to plant turnips or clover on their land at regular intervals. The more efficient use of land freed many farmers to find jobs in cottage industries (based in homes) and eventually to move to the cities, where large mills and weaving establishments were developing.

As the market for British cloth grew, efforts were under way to make the slow process of hand-weaving more efficient. Richard Arkwright had seen James Hargreaves's "spinning jenny"—a multi-spindle machine invented in 1764 for weaving cotton or wool—and noticed the poor quality of the yarn it produced. Using the jenny idea, he developed a spinning table, or "water frame," that could be powered by a horse or by water. He later made the idea popular by building mills using horse-power, then waterpower, and finally steampower to drive the spinning machines.

A major problem in eighteenth-century Britain was excess water in the mines from which iron and coal were dug. Pumping that water out by horse- or manpower was expensive and impractical. However, it was soon discovered that low-grade coal could be used to heat water, producing steam that stored great power. As early as 1712 Thomas Newcomen had begun using steam power to operate mine pumps. James Watt increased the efficiency of the Newcomen "fire engines" (so-named because of the flames that raged beneath the steam boilers) and adapted them for use in factories.

Urbanization. These developments boosted the production of manufactured goods and led to the expansion of cities. In order to market mass-produced materials quickly, improved transportation was necessary; enterprising inventors found ways to build better roads, to outfit locomotives with steam engines, and to power bigger and better ships. Thus the Industrial Revolution was really an evolution of problem-solving ideas.

The Industrial Revolution was driven by the belief that humans were put on earth to conquer it, and could. Change came relatively rapidly because the people of eighteenth-century Britain—already enjoying a high standard of living—demanded even better conditions.

Charles Townshend

1674-1738

Personal Background

Early life. Born in 1674, Charles Townshend was the oldest of three sons of Horatio Townshend, a viscount (nobleman) who had served in the British Parliament. The elder Townshend was one of the richest men in Norfolk, a county in eastern England. As the oldest son, Charles was heir to his father's substantial estate, which was called Raynham. Accordingly, he was provided with the best education possible.

At the age of eleven, Townshend's parents sent him to Eton, a prestigious school for boys preparing for university study. A year later, upon the death of his father, Townshend became the new viscount.

In 1691 Townshend entered King's College at Cambridge University. During his college years, he attended class sporadically and did not pursue a course of study leading to a degree or graduation. Instead, he is said to have spent those years biding his time until he was old enough to take over the responsibilities of his father's title. At Cambridge, he met Robert Walpole, the future prime minister of Britain. Then, after leaving college in 1694, Townshend headed for continental Europe, where he spent the next three years traveling in Holland, France, and Italy.

The young viscount Charles. Along with the title of viscount came a seat in the House of Lords. Upon returning from

▲ **Charles Townshend**

Event: Developing crop rotation.

Role: A wealthy landowner in eastern England, Charles Townshend developed innovative farming methods that included the rotation of crops to improve farm productivity. His work established the foundation for the Industrial Revolution to follow.

mainland Europe in 1697, Townshend assumed his duties in Parliament, at first taking the side of the conservative minority group, the Tories. However, he found that the positions of the Whig party were more to his liking, so he quickly changed parties. (The Whigs, who were then the ruling party in Britain, favored change and reform.) Townshend attended sessions of the House of Lords regularly and served on various committees.

In 1701 Townshend was made lord lieutenant, or chief military officer, of the county of Norfolk. This position allowed him to reward friends and supporters with commissions in the county militia. Townshend remained active in politics and often campaigned for Whig candidates seeking government offices. He later helped his brother Roger win a seat in Parliament.

Marriages. While serving in the House of Lords, Townshend married his first wife, Elizabeth Pelham, daughter of Baron Thomas Pelham. In thirteen years of marriage, the couple had several children; the oldest one, Charles, would become the third Viscount Townshend of Raynham. Elizabeth died in 1712, and Townshend did not remarry until he was fifty-two years old. His second wife, Dorothy Walpole, was the sister of his old school friend Robert.

Diplomat to Holland. All of Townshend's political efforts were rewarded in 1709, when he was sent to Holland as a diplomat to negotiate a treaty with the Dutch. Since 1701 England had been fighting alongside Holland and several other countries against France and Spain in the War of Spanish Succession. While in Holland, Townshend successfully negotiated the "Barrier Treaty," by which England would support Holland's demand for a series of fortified towns in the Spanish Netherlands (now Belgium). Although the terms were later changed, the Barrier Treaty helped bring the war to a close.

Secretary of state. In 1710 the Tories won control of Parliament in a landslide election. The Tory victory cost Townshend his diplomatic post in Holland as well as his title, lord lieutenant. He was not out of power for long, however. When George, the prince of the German state of Hannover, became King George I of England in 1714, Townshend was appointed secretary of state for northern affairs, the highest cabinet post at the time. He was responsible for foreign relations with the nations of northern Europe as well as some domestic affairs. His position also brought him within George's inner circle of advisers.

The always outspoken and opinionated Townshend was soon quarreling with the king over foreign policy. George I maintained close ties to Hannover and wanted England to aid the state in its war with Sweden. Townshend opposed military intervention by Britain in the Baltic region. The dispute cost him the job of secretary of state in 1716, but he was appointed lord lieutenant—George's chief representative—of Ireland.

Five years later, Townshend was again made secretary of state, a post he held until 1730. During the nine years of his second term, he promoted a policy of neutrality in English disputes in the Baltic area and tried to recruit Austria as an ally against France. He also accompanied the king when he made occasional visits to his other court in Hannover.

Retirement from politics. Meanwhile, Robert Walpole had become prime minister of Britain. In the later years of Townshend's term, the two bickered increasingly over English policy. At the same time, Townshend's health was failing. In May 1730 he resigned as secretary of state and lord lieutenant of Ireland and left London to retire to his estate at Raynham. During his convalescence, he made remarkable contributions to the field of agriculture.

Some Descendants of Charles Townshend

Charles Townshend (son): the third viscount of Raynham

Thomas Townshend (son): member of Parliament from Cambridge

George Townshend (son): admiral of the British navy

Charles Townshend (grandson): designer of the famous Townshend Acts that brought on the American Revolution

George Townshend (grandson): the first Marquess Townshend

Thomas Townshend (grandson): Viscount Sydney and secretary of state

---

Participation: Developing Crop Rotation

In eighteenth-century England, most farming was done on small, unconnected strips of land in open fields—a practice dating back to feudal times. Traditionally, farmers planted a wheat crop, followed it with a barley crop, and then left the field fallow, or unplanted, for a year in order to allow the soil to regenerate. Improved farming techniques were gradually introduced in England. As early as the 1640s, Sir Richard Weston, a refugee from the English civil war living in the Spanish Netherlands, noted that farmers improved their harvest by rotating their crops. Instead of letting the fields lie fallow between crops of grain and flax, the farmers planted turnips or clover; this not only replenished the soil but also provided feed for livestock. Weston described his observations in a pamphlet published in England in 1645.

Turnips and clover were introduced into England in the seventeenth century, and soon farmers such as Thomas Coke of Norfolk were experimenting with crop rotation. Jethro Tull, who lived in Townshend's time, used a seed drill to plant turnips instead of scattering the seeds over the whole field. The drill made it possible to plant crops in rows, thereby allowing for cultivation with horse-drawn hoes. Turnips grew well in the sandy soil of Norfolk. Townshend's success with turnip growth on his estate earned him the nickname "Turnip Townshend."

The Townshend estate. Although Townshend inherited a large estate from his father, much of it consisted of rush-covered marshes or sandy wastes that supported a few sheep; it has been described as a place where "two rabbits struggled for every blade of grass" (Prothero, p.174). But Townshend took a keen interest in his land and was determined to enhance its quality and value. In the years before his departure as diplomat to Holland, he prepared the land for cultivation by creating drainage ditches, planting hedges, and fertilizing the soil with marl, a mixture of sand, clay, limestone, and seashell fragments. He is said to have eventually brought four hundred thousand acres under cultivation.

Crop rotation. Townshend became an enthusiastic promoter of crop rotation after his retirement from politics. In lease agreements with tenants who worked portions of his land, Townshend demanded rotation: rye one year; leaving the land fallow a year; then rotating wheat, barley, and oats undersown with clover over the next three years. He also urged tenants to insert a crop of turnips among their grain crops during the rotation.

Townshend's use of lease agreements to promote agricultural improvements was unusual among landowners. According to historian James M. Rosenheim, "His reliance on leases to bring tenants to his view of husbandry was indeed a farsighted innovation and effective strategy" (Rosenheim, p. 154).

Aftermath

Through his ingenious methods, Townshend greatly improved the value of his property. Crop rotation, turnip cultivation, and other agricultural improvements were gradually adopted by Norfolk farmers, though they were slow to spread in surrounding counties. Gradually, however, new agricultural techniques made headway, and by the early nineteenth century farmers using Townshend's methods turned nearby Lincolnshire from rabbit patches and swampland into grain fields and pasture land. The introduction of turnips as livestock feed also improved England's pastoral economy by enabling farmers to feed their sheep during winter.

Townshend spent his last years at his mansion at Raynham with his two unmarried daughters. He died suddenly in June 1738.

For More Information

Prothero, Boland E. *English Farming Past and Present.* London: Longmans, Green, 1912.

Rosenheim, James M. *The Townshends of Raynham.* Middletown, Connecticut: Wesleyan University Press, 1989.

Russell, Sir E. John. *A History of Agricultural Science in Great Britain: 1620-1954.* London: Allen & Unwin, 1966.

Richard Arkwright

1732-1792

Personal Background

Richard Arkwright was born on December 23, 1732, the youngest of thirteen children in a poor family in Preston, Lancashire, in northwestern England. As a child, he received little, if any, schooling. But despite his lack of formal education, he gained a reputation for having a quick mind, a powerful curiosity, and great skill in improving upon the ideas of others.

When he was still in his teens, Arkwright was apprenticed to a barber and learned to make wigs out of human hair. In 1750 he moved to Bolton and joined the established wigmaking company of Edward Pallit. While there, Arkwright developed a method for dyeing hair that was superior to any available at that time. He later sold his secret to other wigmakers, earning enough money to set up his own shop.

Barbering and wigmaking did not provide Arkwright with a sufficient income, so for a time he owned a "public house" (or restaurant and tavern). He married his first wife, Patience Holt, in the mid-1750s. Patience died shortly after giving birth to a son, Richard. Before his death, Arkwright would marry two other women.

Interest in mechanics. Around the time of his second marriage, Arkwright began to experiment with mechanical objects as a hobby. He recognized the need in the blossoming textile industry

▲ Richard Arkwright

Event: Developing an automatic yarn spinning mechanism.

Role: A poor barber and wigmaker with little formal education, Sir Richard Arkwright developed machines and organized factories for the automatic spinning of cotton yarn.

for machines that would accelerate spinning. Cotton manufacture had been introduced into England in the seventeenth century. A hundred years later, yarn spinners were still using distaffs (a staff that holds the unspun cotton) and spinning wheels that dated back to the Middle Ages. This equipment could only spin one strand of yarn at a time. Fifty thousand spinners worked in Lancashire in Arkwright's time and still could not keep up with the demand for yarn from weavers.

Early attempts to speed up spinning. Other inventors had tried with limited success to develop faster ways to spin yarn. In 1738 Lewis Paul and John Wyatt developed a machine that used rollers to spin cotton. Unfortunately, the design was flawed. Twenty-six years later, James Hargreaves invented the "spinning jenny," a hand-operated machine that could spin eight strands of yarn at a time. However, the yarn produced by this machine could only be used for the "woof"—or lateral threads—in cotton cloth. The "warp"—or longitudinal threads—were made from linen, a stronger material.

Participation: Developing Automatic Yarn-Spinning

The "water frame." Around 1766, probably in the course of his own mechanical experiments, Arkwright came to know John Kay, a mechanic and clockmaker. The two men began working together to build a spinning machine. Arkwright spent virtually every spare minute of his time on the project. A working model of the spinning machine was first demonstrated in the home of a local schoolmaster in Preston.

Known as the "water frame" because it was powered by a water wheel, the spinning machine consisted of two pairs of rollers that pulled cotton fibers taut and twisted them into a strong fine thread. The diameter of the thread could be controlled by varying the tension and speed of the rollers.

Organizing factories. Arkwright soon learned that Hargreaves's "spinning jenny" had provoked riots among textile workers, who feared that the machines would put them out of work. In

▲ A replica of Arkwright's 1769 spinning frame; the flyer drew out the thread then twisted it as it was wound onto a spool or bobbin.

1768 he moved to Nottingham, a center of the hosiery industry, where John Smalley, a liquor merchant and painter, and David Thornley joined him as partners. The next year Arkwright took out a patent on the water frame, claiming to be its inventor. He enlisted two stocking manufacturers, Samuel Need and Jedediah

Strut, as financial backers. Together they built a small mill but did not see immediate success.

For the first few years of the mill's operation, the Arkwright family lived in poverty. Nevertheless, Arkwright was determined to expand the business. In 1771 he and his backers decided to build a mill at Cromford in Derbyshire, England. Although Cromford was somewhat isolated, the Derwent River provided water power for the machinery, and the families of local miners offered a potential labor force. The Cromford mill began work in 1772.

Assembly line factories. In an effort to raise his mill's output, Arkwright searched for more efficient ways to process raw cotton. In 1775 he patented a machine that would card (or comb and straighten) cotton by passing it over a roller covered with metal teeth. As the cotton was fed into the machine, the roller combed it into parallel fibers which were then formed into bundles, or rovings, and fed into the water frame to be spun into yarn.

Factory improvements. Gradually, Arkwright's business increased, and he used his profits to build new factories. His prosperity aroused the anxiety of laborers at Birkacre, who in 1779 destroyed one of the mills. That factory was not rebuilt, but others were added to the Arkwright industries. By the next year, he had established mills in Scotland and was selling water frames and carding machines to other businesspeople throughout Britain. Arkwright earned high royalties for the use of the machines under a licensing arrangement.

Arkwright, Hargreaves, and Spinning

One of Arkwright's duties while working for Edward Pallit was to travel around the country buying human hair for wigs. One story credits his interest in spinning to one of these buying trips in the Lancashire area of England. While there, he apparently stopped at the home of James Hargreaves, inventor of the "spinning jenny." It may have been this opportunity to see the "jenny" that inspired Arkwright to work on the "water frame."

Always on the lookout for better ways to spin cotton yarn, Arkwright installed steam engines to power the spinning frames in two of his factories in 1786, after nine years of experimenting with the idea. He arranged for all the operations in the manufacture of cotton yarn to be housed together in one building. Typically, his workers spent thirteen hours a day—six days a week—in the factory and made ten to twelve shillings each week.

Arkwright and the law. As cotton manufacturing expanded during the 1780s, other businesspeople using Arkwright's equipment tried to avoid paying Arkwright royalties. Some simply refused to pay him, while others took out patents for machines similar to those he had patented. Arkwright sued several manufacturers over the use of his milling equipment. He even appealed to the British Parliament for defense of his patents.

Aftermath

Knighthood. Although he eventually lost his carding machine patent and the patent on his water frame expired, Arkwright continued to prosper. He sold his always improving machines and joined in partnerships that gave him controlling interests in several companies. His shrewd business judgment and ability to organize factories and workers provided great success. In 1786 Arkwright was knighted by King George III. That year he began building a mansion, Castle, for his family, which was not completed until 1793, a year after his death.

The Arkwright legacy. Although the ideas behind his machines were not entirely new, Arkwright was the first person to effectively organize the mass production of cotton yarn using machinery. In the words of industrial historian Donald Cardwell: "He understood, as no man had done before, the nature and potential of textile manufacture and he saw clearly how he could harness the new mechanical inventions and create what was essentially a new industry" (Cardwell, p. 144).

Arkwright is credited with establishing a model of a factory system such as the one later developed by Henry Ford at Dearborn, Michigan, for the manufacture of automobiles.

For More Information

Cardwell, Donald. *The Norton History of Technology.* New York: Norton, 1995.

Fitton, R. S. *The Arkwrights: Spinners of Fortune.* Manchester, England: Manchester University Press, 1989.

Lipson, E. *The History of the Woolen and Worsted Industries.* London: Frank Cass & Co., 1965.

James Watt

1736-1819

Personal Background

Early life. James Watt was born January 19, 1736, in the small town of Greenock, Scotland. His father made a living however he could in this sparsely populated nation, working variously as a merchant, a carpenter, and a government administrator. Young James frequently assisted his father as a carpenter and from an early age enjoyed carpenter's tools more than books.

Education. As a child, Watt was physically weak and experienced long periods of illness. For that reason, he did not begin his education at the usual age. Even when he did enroll in school, illness frequently kept him from class. However, Watt demonstrated a keen ability to learn on his own. As he played with carpenter's tools, he learned and applied mathematical concepts.

In his teens, Watt was sent to a commercial school, where he studied Latin, Greek, and mathematics. At home, he experimented with chemicals and created new tools. By the age of fifteen, he had found a way to make a simple electric motor.

Watt spent a year at the University of Glasgow in Scotland, where he studied to become a mathematical instrument-maker. He then moved to London and worked for a man named John Morgan, making accurate quadrants (tools for measuring the altitude of stars) and parallel rulers.

▲ **James Watt**

Event: Providing steam power for British factories.

Role: An engineering genius, James Watt refined existing steam engines to improve their functions. His efforts contributed to the rise of large-scale mills and factories.

▲ Watt's first "sun and planet" steam engine, now in the Science Museum in London, England.

"Inventor" of the steam engine. Watt returned to Scotland when he was twenty. He took a job at the University of Glasgow, cleaning and repairing scientific instruments. While working there, he developed an interest in steam power. Though Watt is often credited with "inventing" the steam engine—and he certainly deserves credit for making steam power popular and for adapting it to many uses—other innovators had experimented with steam power earlier. Steam engines were already in operation in many mining areas of England, where they powered pumps to keep the mines from flooding. One of the chief builders of workable steam pumps was Thomas Newcomen. After cleaning and repairing the university's model of a Newcomen steam engine, Watt became fascinated with the idea of improving steam power.

Watt recognized the weaknesses of the Newcomen "fire engines." He was still working at the university when he thought of a way to produce energy more efficiently:

> It was in the Green of Glasgow. I had gone to take a walk on a fine Sabbath afternoon.... I was thinking upon the engine at the time and had gone as far as the Herd's house when the idea came into my mind, that as steam was an elastic body it would rush into a vacuum, and if a communication was made between cylinder and an exhausted vessel, it would rush into it, and might be there condensed without cooling the cylinder.... I had not walked further than the Golf-house when the whole thing was arranged in my mind. (Watt in Storer, p. 52)

The next day, Watt began working on a model of his new engine. He added a separate condenser to the Newcomen model, thereby allowing the "fire engine" to stay hot without a period of cooling. This way a large pump could be driven faster than Newcomen's twelve strokes a minute.

The Watt mind. It took nearly ten years—until May 1775—before a real working-size model of Watt's engine was ready. (Watt had a habit of flitting from one project to another and was simultaneously working on the invention of a copying machine and a steam dryer.) He obtained a patent on the basis of his first model for the new engine in 1769, but he still had not developed a full-scale engine four years later.

A new partnership. In the late 1760s Watt entered a partnership with Dr. John Roebuck, owner of Carron Ironworks. By 1773, however, the Roebuck-Watt partnership was on shaky ground. Roebuck's ironworks were in financial trouble, and a new group of investors offered to take the Watt project off Roebuck's hands.

The Fire Engine

Because Newcomen replaced manpower or horsepower with the force of steam from a huge boiler heated by burning coal, his machines were first known as "fire engines." They were popular in one of England's largest industries, coal mining, because of the ready availability of low-grade coal that needed to be burned up.

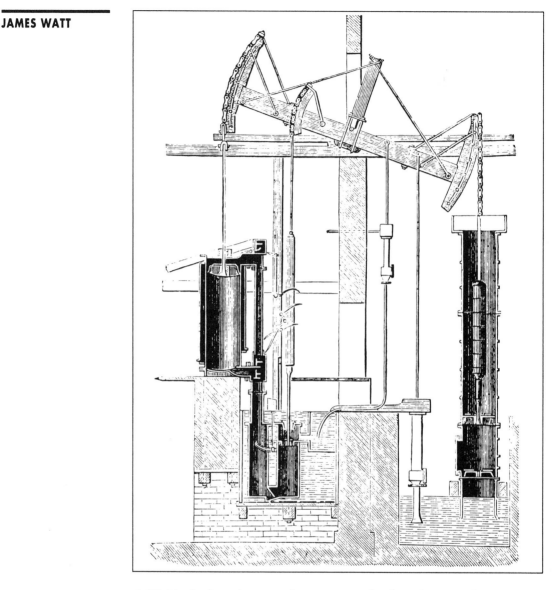

▲ Watt's single-acting pumping steam engine for mines, 1769; steam engines were used in many mining areas of England to power pumps to keep the mines from flooding.

Matthew Boulton, the owner of a toolmaking firm, became Watt's new partner. Boulton had the experience needed to produce cylinders and pistons (sliding cylindrical valves) for steam engines. In 1775 Boulton sold several of the engines to operate water pumps, and the next year two of them were installed in coal mines.

Popularizing the steam engine. Over the next fifteen years, Watt continued to work on various improvements to the steam engine. He turned it upside down, making a "topsy turvy" model that could operate a pump directly without the need for a large and cumbersome rocker arm; he found a way to turn the engine on its side so that it could be used in other factory activities; and he created the first steam valve that would allow steam to apply force on either side of the piston alternately. Watt later invented a series of gears called the "sun and planet" to change the push-pull motion of the engine to circular motion used to power mills.

Aftermath

At age sixty-four Watt sold his interests in the company to his son, James. By that time, he had demonstrated the usefulness of steam power to drive many kinds of industrial machines. His inventions fueled the Industrial Revolution in Great Britain, resulting in the production of a wide variety of goods that could be sold in Britain's markets around the world. At the same time, other inventors were attempting to power automobiles with steam engines.

In spite of his success, Watt is said to have been melancholy and withdrawn by nature. He had warm friendships but hated to meet face to face with anyone in business negotiations. In his old age, however, he demonstrated a desire to share his knowledge and reminisce about his past successes. The *watt,* a metric unit of power, is named for him.

For More Information

Holt, L. T. C. *Thomas Newcomen: The Prehistory of the Steam Engine.* London: Dawlish MacDonald, 1963.

Smiles, S. *Lives of Boulton and Watt.* London: Murray, 1865.

Storer, J. D. *A Simple History of the Steam Engine.* London: John Baker, 1969.

Bibliography

Aaron, Richard. *John Locke*. Oxford: Clarendon, 1973.

Amon, Richard Athama. *John Locke*. 3rd ed. Oxford: Clarendon Press, 1973.

Armitage, Angus. *John Kepler*. New York: Ray, 1966.

Arnesen, Peter Judd. *The Medieval Japanese Daimyo*. New Haven, Connecticut: Yale University Press, 1970.

Artz, F. *The Enlightenment in France*. Kent, Ohio: Kent State University Press, 1968.

Bacon, Sir Francis. *The Works of Francis Bacon*. Edited by J. Spedding. London: Longmans, Green, 1861.

Boxer, Charles R. *The Christian Century in Japan*. Berkeley: University of California Press, 1974.

Byron, William. *Cervantes: A Biography*. Garden City, New York: Doubleday, 1978.

Cannavaggio, Jean. *Cervantes*. New York: Norton, 1990.

Cervantes, Miguel de. *Don Quixote*. New York: Washington Square Press, 1957.

Chute, Marchette. *Shakespeare of London*. New York: Dutton, 1949.

Clark, William R. *Explorers of the World*. London: Aldus Books Ltd., 1964.

Coleridge, Hartley. *Biographia Borealis: Lives of Distinguished Northerners*. London: Whittaker, Treacher and Co., 1833.

Cooke, Jacob Ernest. *Encyclopedia of North American Colonies*. New York: Scribner, 1993.

dos Passos, John. *The Portugal Story*. New York: Doubleday, 1969.

Dower, John W. *Japanese History and Culture from Ancient to Modern Times: Seven Basic Biographies*. New York: Weiner, 1986.

Ellis, Edward S., and Charles F. Horne. *The World's Famous Events*. Vol. 3. New York: Francis R. Niglutsch, 1913.

Hall, John Whitney, Nagahara Keiji, and Kozo Yamamura, editors. *Japan Before Tokugawa: Political Consolidation and Economic Growth, 1500-1650*. Princeton, New Jersey: Princeton University Press, 1981.

Hatton, Ragnhold. *George I—Elector and King*. Cambridge, Massachusetts: Harvard University Press, 1978.

Herrman, Paul. *The Great Age of Discovery*. New York: Harper, 1958.

Knight, David C. *Johannes Kepler and Planetary Motion*. New York: Watts, 1962.

Ledesma, Francisco Navarro. *Cervantes: The Man and the Genius*. New York: Charterhouse, 1973.

BIBLIOGRAPHY

Lloyd, Sarah. *An Indian Attachment.* New York: Morrow, 1984.

McLeod, W. H. *The Sikhs: History, Religion, and Society.* New York: Columbia University Press, 1989.

Neal, Henry Edward. *From Spinning Wheel to Spacecraft.* New York: Julian Messner, 1964.

Riches, Naomi. *The Agricultural Revolution in Norfolk.* London: Frank Case & Co., 1967.

Ronan, Colin, and Joseph Needham. *The Shorter Science and Civilisation in China.* 3 vols. Cambridge, England: Cambridge University Press, 1981.

Rosen, Sidney. *The Harmonious World of Johann Kepler.* Boston: Little, Brown, 1962.

Rousseau, Jean-Jacques. *The Social Contract and Discourses.* Translated by G. D. H. Cole. New York: Dutton, 1950.

Russell, B. *A History of Western Philosophy.* New York: Simon & Schuster, 1945.

Sarton, G. *Six Wings: Men of Science in the Renaissance.* Bloomington: Indiana University Press, 1957.

Schiffler, H. *The Quest for Africa.* New York: Putnam, 1957.

Spielvogel, Jackson J. *Western Civilization.* 2 vols. St. Paul, Minnesota: West Publishing Co., 1994.

Syme, Ronald. *Cartier: Finder of the St. Lawrence.* New York: Morrow, 1958.

Tacket, T. *Priest and Parish in Eighteenth-Century France.* Princeton, New Jersey: Princeton University Press, 1977.

Trudel, Marcel. *Dictionary of Canadian Biography.* Vol 1. Toronto: University of Toronto Press, 1966.

Voltaire. *The Portable Voltaire.* Edited by Ben Ray Redman. New York: Viking, 1968.

Wilson, Arthur M. *Diderot.* New York: Oxford University Press, 1972.

Winmar, Frances. *Jean-Jacques Rousseau: Conscience of an Era.* New York: Random House, 1961.

Wright, Louis B., editor. *Shakespeare's England.* New York: Harper, 1964.

Index

Bold indicates entries and their page numbers; (ill.) indicates illustrations.

℘ROFILES IN WORLD HISTORY

Significant Events and the People Who Shaped Them